Creative Native American Beading

THERESA FLORES GEARY, Ph.D.

Sterling Publishing Co., Inc.
New York

Edited by Jeanette Green
Designed by Judy Morgan
Ellen Liberles project consultant
Chapter-open photos by Nancy Palubniak
Step photos by Debra Whalen of Photographic Works
Basic stitch drawings by Kim Coxey of Chapelle, Ltd.
Patterns and graphs by the author

Library of Congress Cataloging-in-Publication Data
Geary, Theresa Flores.
  Creative native American beading / Theresa Flores Geary.
      p. cm.
  Includes index.
  ISBN 1-4027-1077-1
  1. Beadwork—Patterns. 2. Indian beadwork—North America. I. Title.

TT860.G4297 2005
745.58'2—dc22   2004020304

2   4   6   8   10   9   7   5   3

Published by Sterling Publishing Co., Inc.
387 Park Avenue South, New York, NY 10016
© 2005 by Theresa Flores Geary
Distributed in Canada by Sterling Publishing
℅ Canadian Manda Group, 165 Dufferin Street
Toronto, Ontario, Canada M6K 3H6
Distributed in the United Kingdom by GMC Distribution Services,
Castle Place, 166 High Street, Lewes, East Sussex, England BN7 1XU
Distributed in Australia by Capricorn Link (Australia) Pty. Ltd.
P.O. Box 704, Windsor, NSW 2756, Australia

Sterling ISBN-13: 978-1-4027-1077-3
        ISBN-10: 1-4027-1077-1

For information about custom editions, special sales, premium and
corporate purchases, please contact Sterling Special Sales
Department at 800-805-5489 or specialsales@sterlingpub.com.

For my father, Joe Flores, an exceptional man

ACKNOWLEDGMENTS

I would like to express my sincere appreciation for the beadwork pattern designers and beaders who contributed to this book. They include Angelique Alvarez, Heather Bacon, Sylvia Elam, Genny Hatathlie, Eric Johnson, Louise Johnson, Cherri Miller, Lula Monroe, Jonathan M. Pulley, and Shelia Vinson.

I would like to thank Hasha, who taught Deb Weinman, who in turn helped me fine-tune my techniques on increasing and decreasing peyote stitch for making exquisite beaded vases. I am very grateful to all my teachers, past and present, and to all my students who have demanded that I learn advanced techniques so that I could teach them. I also would like to acknowledge the authors, bead-pattern designers, store owners, wholesalers, dealers, bead manufacturers, and beaders who help keep the art of beadwork alive for future generations.

I also need to acknowledge my editor, Jeanette Green, who is a master at putting together a wonderful book, and all the staff at Sterling Publishing Co., Inc., who provide amazing support to produce a beautiful quality publication. In addition, I would like to honor both Nancy Palubniak and Deb Whalen for their excellent photography and appreciation of small things of beauty.

Finally, I thank my family who have faithfully tolerated my mood swings and provided invaluable technical assistance with computer software/hardware issues, photography, and editing.

—Theresa Flores Geary

CONTENTS

Introduction

What's usually referred to as Native American beadwork is the style of beadwork seen in literature and museums that's particular to Native Americans. However, contemporary beadwork takes the Native style out of history books and places it in modern times. Today Native American beaders have the advantage of using modern tools and materials for their artwork. In earlier times, Native beaders often worked on leather. Although leather is a supple fabric, it's not comparable to synthetics, such as Ultrasuede, through which a needle easily glides as though the fabric were butter. Anyone who has sewn beads onto leather knows that it tortures both your fingers and your needles. Before fine beading needles were manufactured, beaders used natural materials, such as yucca needles and animal sinew for thread, to create their art.

Certain artistic themes have dominated traditional and contemporary Native beadwork, and the older labor-intensive beadwork remains highly valued. Unlike the incredible museum specimens, such as knee-high beaded moccasins, beaded cradleboards, or beaded wedding dresses, most projects in this book can be completed in a weekend or less. Few modern beaders have the time or inclination to undertake laborious projects. Some Native beaders prefer traditional beadwork that involves symbolic or ceremonial objects to contemporary designs. Others draw on traditional symbols or themes and rework them into artworks favored by the contemporary marketplace.

This book draws on many different Native beading techniques and themes. The projects are not all-inclusive, nor are they authoritative on the Native beadwork style, but they are meant to honor both the art form and the artists. The main purpose of each project is to teach various beading techniques and to inspire creative ways of using colors, components, and materials to make objects of beauty.

Here we'll show you how to make many different types of beaded projects, ranging from those intended for beginners to those more advanced. We note the skill level required for each project at the beginning of each chapter. If you are a novice with no experience but love beadwork, you'll find several projects that are easy to complete without much pain. After you have completed a few projects, you'll gain more confidence and be able to tackle intermediate projects. You may be surprised to find that you are more advanced in your knowledge than you realize. Many people with experience in other arts and crafts techniques, such as the sewing arts—crochet, knitting, needlepoint, and embroidery—have skills that easily transfer into beadwork skills.

Pink and yellow earrings using the Huichol stitch by Angelique Alvarez.

HOW TO READ BEADING PATTERNS

Beading patterns are not difficult to read as long as you understand a few things about different techniques and stitches. If a pattern dictates that you begin at the top or the bottom, the right or the left side, it's usually a good idea to follow the pattern-maker's suggestion.

However, most of us are oriented to be right-hand dominant or left-hand dominant. Some versatile folks have mixed dominance. Visual perception may also be right- or left-dominant; you may favor your right or left eye. Those lucky ambidextrous people can use either hand equally well. Without becoming too technical, I usually observe students and advise them to use the hand and direction that feels most comfortable. Most right-handed people feel comfortable beading from right to left and top to bottom.

Even so, no rule prevents you from beading from bottom to top or left to right. In fact, I generally recommend that students try beading in the opposite direction from what they're most used to in order to exercise their brains. Some find that the opposite direction is actually easier for them.

Apache-Weave Patterns
Unless a pattern specifies exactly where to start, you can generally begin anywhere you choose. Projects in Chapters 3 to 7 and 16 all use Apache-weave patterns. Apache weave is also called brick stitch or stacking stitch. It has also been called Comanche or Cheyenne weave. The arrow on the accompanying pattern(s) tells you where to start so that your work will be coordinated with the project step photos.

Many patterns for Apache-weave earrings advise that you start at the widest point, as suggested in Chapter 16. This is usually a good rule of thumb. The reason for this is that the basic Apache weave automatically decreases with each row. Apache weave is used in the popular triangle-shaped earrings with fringe. Since the stitch automatically decreases with each new row, your beadwork will look like a triangle. When you finish one triangle and then the bottom half, your beadwork will be diamond-shaped.

Notice that the gecko vest pattern in Chapter 16 is perfectly symmetrical, which means that the top half of the pattern is the same as the bottom half. When the first half is completed, you will weave your thread to the base or starting row, then turn your work upside down and finish the bottom half. If you started anywhere else in the pattern, you would need to increase, which involves a little more effort.

Many experienced beaders do not know how to increase with Apache weave. This book teaches the increasing Apache weave (increasing brick stitch) since it makes the stitch more versatile. In addition, increasing allows a beader to produce many different shapes other than the triangle or diamond, as seen in Chapters 7 and 18 projects. Round or circular Apache weave (round or circular brick stitch) is slightly different due to its three-dimensionality. Most patterns that use this stitch tell you where to begin for the easiest way to follow the pattern.

Gecko vest pattern

Round or Circular Peyote-Stitch Patterns

Round or circular peyote stitch is a three-dimensional technique. While the pattern is flat or two-dimensional, the beadwork will become a three-dimensional circle or ring of beads. At the end of each you'll need to "drop down" or "step up" to begin the next row. These terms actually mean the same thing, depending on whether you're working the pattern beginning from the top or

Turtle pot using the round peyote pattern

from the bottom. If you turn your work upside down, you'll see that it is actually the same.

Since you are either stepping up or dropping down at the end of each row, you will notice that the first bead of each row actually shifts by one bead every row. Some patterns will note this by having a red line drawn through the pattern to mark the shift. However, this is difficult for many beaders to understand. I advise my students to look at the beadwork to see that it looks the same as the pattern. Of course, we need to translate that two-dimensional pattern into a three-dimensional beaded image.

Notice that the beaded hatband in Chapter 6 does not tell you where to begin. The project is three-dimensional, and the first half is a mirror image of the second half. Thus, you could start at the top or the bottom and the result would be the same.

The patterns for miniature pottery in Chapter 1 are slightly different because the pots are not identical in shape or size. The project calls for increasing the number of beads at strategic points to accommodate the size and curve of the pottery. To attach your beads to the pottery, you begin at the neck of the pottery using background beads. You then add

Kokopelli Copper Bag

and back are identical or mirror images. The thunderbird design is asymmetrical since the front side is completely different from the back side.

Flat Peyote-Stitch Patterns

Since the flat peyote stitch is two-dimensional, it is often easier to follow a pattern than for either the round or circular peyote stitch. If the pattern has only one color, as does the slide in the hatband project in Chapter 6, you can start from either the right or the left side. The beadwork is then curved into a circular shape and seamed up the side with a technique called a zipper stitch. Most of the patterns included in this book show photos of the steps with a right-to-left orientation. However, with flat peyote stitch, you bead from right to left and then change directions with each row. You do not need to turn your work over to begin the next row. Just continue beading each row and position your hands to comfortably change directions.

Chapter 12 features an odd-count peyote-stitch pattern. Sometimes a pattern dictates the use of an odd number of beads instead of an even number to produce the proper symmetry of the design. Here the odd-count flat-peyote turnaround is used in every other row. If you design your own patterns and do not have a good reason for doing odd-count, try even-count since it's easier for most people to bead. Also remember that if you're not careful with your thread tension, the edges will not be straight.

WHAT YOU'LL NEED FOR BEADING

To acquire a working knowledge of beading techniques and materials, refer to the glossary (page 119). Each chapter has specific recommendations for materials to use for each project. Since it's helpful to have basic information on materials, here are a few notes. With experience you'll learn what threads, needles, and beads help create the nicest piece of beadwork.

your pattern beads against the solid background beads. Your increases are placed only within the background beads and not in the pattern itself. As indicated in the project, you can place one or several patterns on the same pot. Another example is the turtle pattern in Chapter 11.

Chapter 11 features several patterns in the peyote stitch. Notice that the pink cross and *ojo de Dios* patterns are symmetrical, which means that the front

Colors When choosing color combinations, you might want to look at other people's beadwork, check out jewelry-store displays, or thumb through magazines or books. If what you see appeals to you, try choosing similar colors. If you have difficulty creating your own color combinations, consult a color wheel and learn the basics of color matching. Colors recommended for these projects are meant only as suggestions. You're encouraged to try out different colors that suit your personality.

Delicas and Color Numbers Where color numbers are included, they refer to Delicas, standardized colors manufactured of a Japanese bead noted for precise shaping and larger holes. They may be noted as DB# by stores. Since they've been cut with lasers, Delicas are very consistent in size and popular with modern beaders. Delica is a trademark of Miyuki Shoji Corp. The term *cylinder* refers to the shape of the bead commonly known as Delicas.

Seed Beads Seed beads come in standardized sizes ranging from size 8 to 15. While there are beads smaller than 15's, they are difficult to find. Also, not all bead manufacturers have precise cutting techniques, so the sizing does not always match completely. Beginners may need a magnifying glass to see the differences. *The larger the size number, the smaller the bead.* For example, a size 15 is smaller than a size 8. A reputable bead dealer will tell you the name of the manufacturer and where the beads were manufactured. Seed-bead sizes are based on external dimensions, not the size of the hole.

Bead Selection Choosing beads can be confusing for beginners. The easiest way to guarantee size consistency is to use the same type of bead for a particular project and to avoid mixing manufacturers. When beads of different manufacturers are mixed, the results can be lumpy and uneven. For example, Japanese beads tend to be more square than beads made in the Czech Republic, which tend to be more oval. Both nations produce good-quality beads, so

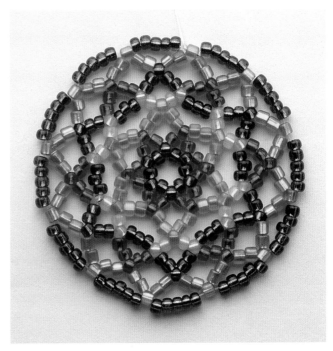

Huichol lace sun catcher, chapter 13.

choose the shape you prefer. Czech beads are usually strung on hanks, and Japanese beads are usually sold in tubes. Japanese beads tend to have larger holes than Czech beads. The colors are not standardized among manufacturers.

Bead Finishes The many available bead finishes produce an elaborate selection of gorgeous and exotic beads you can use for beading projects. Some finishes are vulnerable to wear, depending on your personal body chemistry or exposure to hand lotions and perfumes. If a bead is marked as dyed, the finish could rub off and ruin your beadwork. Metallicized or galvanized beads also have this tendency. Acrylic products can be sprayed or painted on beadwork to reduce the problem. Consult personnel at your local bead store to determine whether the color is stable so that you can make an informed decision.

Beading Needles Various countries and manufacturers produce beading needles. These needles are different from sewing needles because the eye tends to be smaller since it needs to accommodate the size of the bead hole. The size of beading needle usually coincides with the bead size. For instance, a size 10 beading needle works well with a size 10 bead. However, many people do not know that beading needles are somewhat versatile because the hole size is more important than the bead size. I usually recommend a size 10 needle for size 10, 11, and 12 beads. I consider this a good generic size because it works well with many beads and projects. If you begin working with size 12 or 13 beads, I recommend a size 12 needle. Antique beads tend to have smaller holes than the beads currently manufactured.

Beading Thread Beading thread comes in many sizes, based on the width of the individual piece of

This brooch or pin uses appliqué stitch in combination with black onyx, carnelian, and turquoise cabochons to create a more free-form piece of jewelry. Chapter 4.

thread. It differs from sewing thread in that it is more durable and less likely to have natural components. Synthetics like polyester and nylon have a longer life span than cotton or silk, which will biodegrade in 50 years or less. If you want your beadwork to become a family heirloom or to retire someday into a museum, consider the thread's life span. The most commonly available threads are, from small to large, A, O, B, and D. Consider the weight factor of glass beads. You may need to use size D thread for a loomed belt or other heavy piece of beadwork. Sizes A or O are generally recommended for lightweight and delicate beadwork, such as earrings. Size B is recommended more for small but slightly heavier beadwork pieces like bracelets and necklaces.

Different thread manufacturers compete to produce quality products in a variety of colors besides black and white. Some beading threads are conditioned with a type of waxy or slippery material to minimize fraying and tangling. Beeswax and other thread conditioners can help if you have that problem.

Another factor to consider in choosing the thread size is how many times a piece of thread needs to pass through a single bead. If you're using a stitch that requires more than two passes of thread, you may have to use a finer thread size. If the only thread you have is too thin to fill the bead hole, you can double your thread and save yourself a trip to the bead store.

Threading the Needle The amount of thread to use is based partly on the project. However, as a general rule of thumb, I usually recommend an arm's length doubled. Even though you may be using only a single thread, you can double the thread back on itself to shorten it to a comfortable length. The thread length will be awkward and tangle easily if it is longer than your arm can reach. If you need more thread, it's easy to tie it off and add a new piece of thread. It is important to know that the thread should be put into your needle in the

HELPFUL HINTS

Beading is a very creative activity. For beginners, it's helpful to have some basic structure and simple rules. However, after you gain a little experience and confidence, you'll learn that there are many different ways to attach beads together with some sort of stringing material. Many different techniques can achieve the same result. If you find it difficult to learn the round peyote stitch, you may discover that you can achieve the same results by making a flat piece of beadwork with flat peyote stitch and then seaming both ends to make a tubular piece of beadwork. Flat peyote stitch looks the same as Apache weave (brick stitch) turned sideways. Loomed beadwork looks the same as square-stitch beadwork.

I recommend that beginners start with beginner projects and master one technique at a time. After you understand how beads behave, it will be much easier to adapt a particular project to achieve individual results. Even though certain materials are recommended for each project, it's helpful to remember that many other materials can also be used. Some materials may not be available in local bead or craft stores, although I did choose supplies that are readily available in most large cities. If necessity dictates that you substitute certain materials, such as larger beads than what are recommended here, you might be pleasantly surprised at the results. Be creative, explore the many different options, and see what happens.

We show drawings of the basic stitch(es) used in the project chapter at the beginning of each chapter. Remember, you'll find these stitches and other helpful beading terms in the glossary.

Blue violet flowerpot from chapter 9.

same direction as it comes off the spool, to prevent tangling and fraying.

Beading Supplies You can find more information about where to buy beads and other beading materials in your local telephone directory, by browsing in bead and craft stores, and by searching for stores and suppliers on the Internet.

Knots We've included drawings of basic knots, like the square knot, in-line or half-hitch knot, and surgeon's knot in the glossary.

"A hundred times every day I remind myself that my inner and outer life depend on the labors of other men, living and dead, and that I must exert myself in order to give in the same measure as I have received and am still receiving."

—Albert Einstein

1 Rock-Art Pottery

ROUND PEYOTE STITCH

ADVANCED

In strange contrast to the urban sprawl of Phoenix, Arizona, the South Mountains form a rugged landscape looming 1,500 feet above the surrounding desert. These mountains contain a wealth of carvings called petroglyphs, chiseled into rock. Scientists and anthropologists have concluded that the rock art, created by ancient Native peoples, dates as far back as the eighth century.

The subjects of rock art include insects, arthropods, amphibians, reptiles, mammals, birds, humans, and geometric designs. Some sites have panels of images, rather than isolated ones, that suggest spiritual journeys, historical events, or significant memories.

Although various theories explain the individual meanings of these images, most interpretations derive from ethnographic knowledge from living cultures of Native peoples in the Southwest. Native informants believe that the site was used for vision quests and that the art reveals a pictorial representation of spiritual journeys. Anthropologists have also concluded that rock art expresses shamanistic visual images associated with travels into the Other World. Others have speculated that the rock art has maps or sacred geography, shows spirit beings, reveals animal transformations, or describes life energy, flight, and solar events.

Humans try to understand and interpret the sacred territory of dreams, visions, memories, and other phenomena of the natural and spiritual world that help explain our relation to the universe. Certain locations reveal either a shadow or sun rays on a rock to indicate a seasonal change like the summer and winter solstice that marks the longest and shortest days of the year.

Rock art characteristically uses simple stick figures or line drawings with little attention to detail. Many four-legged rock-art mammals are anatomically incorrect and disproportionate, contrary to the evidence that ancient artists could also produce meticulously detailed artwork.

Anthropologists use the term *anthropomorphs* for humanlike figures, although many speculate that the figures may represent either humans or spirits. Some figures are notably wearing headdresses or holding an object in the hand, such as a staff or cane. Other images of humans share animal features.

The hummingbird, a notable symbol in Aztec tradition, often appears with an ancient warrior known for wearing a hummingbird helmet. Reportedly, the hummingbird has become a symbol of rejuvenation or resurrection. It has beautiful iridescent coloring and is one of the world's smallest birds. Because of its light-reflective coloring, it is also known as a sun creature. In spite of its size, the hummingbird can be quite aggressive and territorial. Birds in general symbolize spiritual transformation and flight into the supernatural world.

A maze represents the path of life or the Creator's plan for our spiritual journey on this earth. Other geometric shapes may reflect the powers of nature or the movement of celestial beings.

With a little exploration, you'll find rock art fascinating at the very least.

Rock-art images are a good source of inspiration for beadwork designs. Only a few patterns are offered in this chapter for you to explore. If you research the subject, you'll be able to find more photographs and reproductions of other images to aid your own interpretation. Other suggested uses for rock-art designs include beaded rocks, earrings, storytelling panels, and loomed strips.

MATERIALS

- small terra-cotta pottery or glass vase, 1 to 1½ inches high

- size 14 beads, two contrasting colors

- size A or O beading thread

- size 12 beading needle

BASIC STITCH

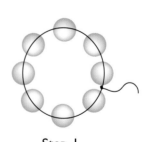

Step 1

Round Peyote Stitch

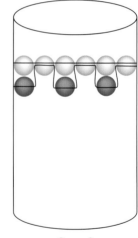

Step 2

Project Notes This project uses the round or circular peyote stitch to cover an irregular three-dimensional object. A small pottery or glass vase with a lip will help prevent the beads from sliding off when you begin the project. As the shape flares out, it will be necessary to increase the number of beads in strategic locations to accommodate the shape changes. As the shape turns in or gets smaller, you will have to decrease the number of beads you use.

To make a smoothly beaded surface, you'll need to follow a few simple rules. First, plan your increases to be placed in the background rather than in the design itself. Second, space your increases evenly throughout the circumference of the pottery or vase and not right next to each other. Third, use a relaxed tension so that you will notice when the thread gaps require an increase.

The round peyote stitch is also called the circular increasing and decreasing peyote stitch.

1. Tie a ring of beads to fit loosely around the top edge of the pottery. A gap that's one or two beads wide will allow the beads to be evenly spaced around the circumference with a tiny amount of thread showing between the beads.

2. Add one bead every other bead. If you are using an even number of beads, you will need to "drop down" at the end of each row by passing your needle through the first bead of row 1 and down through the first bead added. If you are using an odd number of beads, the rows will spiral indefinitely with no beginning or end to the rows. The photo below shows the drop-down step.

3. Continue adding beads until you see the need to increase for a good fit. Increasing is a two-step process. Add as many increases as necessary on that row, depending on whether the increase in the size of the pottery is gradual or radical. First, add two beads in the place where you usually add one bead. Second, when you get all the way around the row to the two-bead increase, add one bead between each bead and continue beading as usual.

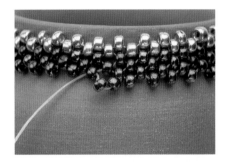

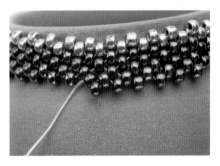

4. When your pottery shape reduces in size, you will need to decrease the beads by passing your thread through two beads instead of just one.

5. Follow one or more of the pattern designs that we've provided and fill in the background with a contrasting color. Depending on the size of your pottery, it may be able to accommodate two to three designs.

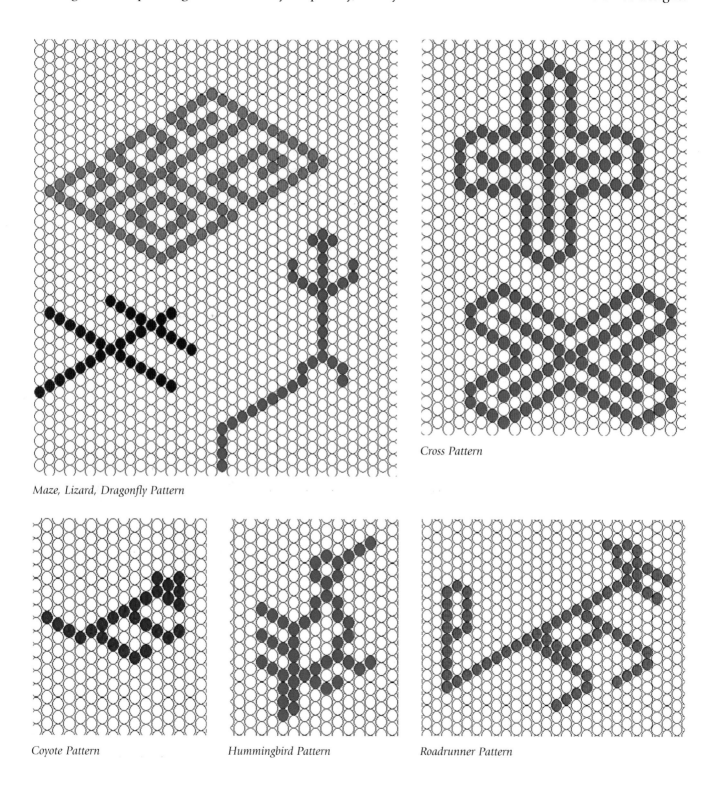

Maze, Lizard, Dragonfly Pattern

Cross Pattern

Coyote Pattern

Hummingbird Pattern

Roadrunner Pattern

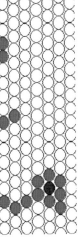

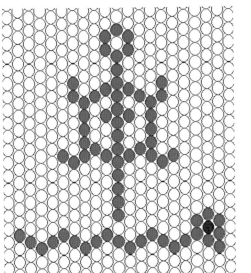

Turtle Pattern

Diamond Maze Pattern

VARIATIONS

Here are a few of the rock-art designs beaded around pots—the cross, hummingbird, maze, and coyote.

Cross Pot

Maze Pot

Hummingbird Pot

Coyote Pot

2

Badge-Holder Necklace

STRINGING

BEGINNER

*M*any employers have their employees or visitors wear badges for identification and security. Here's where a badge-holder necklace comes in handy. Why not make this functional neck strap, typically made out of plastic or inexpensive cord, beautiful?

Some tribes like using their tribal colors to identify with their local community and to show their cultural pride. Similar to the colors of red, white, and blue used by the United States as a symbol of patriotism, many tribes have recognized tribal colors, each representing different things. For example, the Yaqui tribe has a flag with bands of red, white, and sky blue, adorned with a cross, moon, sun, and stars. The color white symbolizes the purity of spirit, the blue symbolizes the sky, and red symbolizes the blood shed to protect the people as well as their land, customs, and religion.

This project is fairly simple for a beginner, but it is also very appropriate for people with physical limitations.

This project has been used in a service program designed to offer a social support system for elderly Native women receiving dialysis. The women suffer from a medical condition that is very challenging because it limits daily activities. Many of these elderly women have seriously impaired vision and arthritis which limits their psychomotor strength and coordination. The stiff beading wire used in this necklace makes it easier for them to string beads. Trays with separate compartments help them keep the colors separate if they cannot see well enough to discriminate between the colors. The beading activity allows the women to socialize and keeps them involved with their families and communities. They also enjoy the added benefit of selling their badge holders to community members and reaping the financial rewards for their creative labor. This also makes a great project for youngsters in after-school programs and for fund-raisers.

MATERIALS

- 1 yard bead-stringing wire, gauge 18, 20, or 22

- 1 ounce of pony beads, one or two colors

- assorted accent beads (gemstone, glass, metal, bone)

- badge clip (available in office supply stores)

- 2 crimper beads

- crimper tool or flat-nose jewelry pliers

- wire-cutting tool or nail clippers

- adhesive tape

Project Notes The badge holders we show have two different types of badge clips. They can be either strung on or held on with a metal snap. Several different designs have the same effect of attaching your badge to a necklace, and some can be worn without a badge clip. Of course, if you have no use for a badge, you can simply make the necklace.

1. Begin your project by placing a piece of adhesive tape at one end of the wire to prevent beads from falling off. String 5 pony beads and 1 crimper bead on your wire first. Finish stringing the length of the necklace with any pattern that you find aesthetically pleasing. Finish the beading by adding 1 crimper bead and 5 pony beads. Leave at least 3 inches of wire on each end for finishing.

2. Cross the wires so that they each exit through a crimper bead. Thread one wire end through the 5 pony beads on the other wire and coming out of the crimper bead. Thread the second wire through 5 pony beads and the crimper bead of the first wire. Both wires now cross and there are 10 pony beads in between.

3. Crimp each crimper bead by applying pressure on the bead with the crimper tool or needle-nose pliers. Crimper beads are made of specially designed soft metal that collapses easily with pressure. Test your crimp to guarantee a secure hold.

4. Trim the wire tails with wire cutters.

5. Attach the badge clip, and your necklace is ready to wear.

VARIATIONS

The Yaqui badge-holder necklace (below left) can be worn without the badge clip for a community celebration.

The badge-holder necklace (right) was created with peyote-stitch beadwork. A badge holder with a solid beadwork rope commands a high price due to the labor-intensive nature of the stitch.

3 White Buffalo Calf Earrings

APACHE WEAVE AND FLAT PEYOTE STITCH

INTERMEDIATE

In his book, The Sacred Pipe: Black Elk's Account of the Seven Rites of the Oglala Sioux, *Black Elk recounts the true story of the White Buffalo Calf Woman. This small project pattern is offered as a remembrance of a highly significant event.*

As the story is told, two hunters spotted a very beautiful woman wearing white buckskin and carrying a bundle on her back. As she approached, one of the men had lustful thoughts and spoke of his desires. The other man cautioned him not to speak so disrespectfully because she was surely a sacred or holy woman. As the mysterious woman approached, they were both covered in a cloud. As soon as the cloud lifted, the "bad" man was reduced to a pile of bones crawling with snakes. She told the "good" man that she had a message to deliver to their chief, Standing Hollow Horn.

She delivered to the chief a bundle which when unwrapped revealed the sacred pipe. She offered the pipe as a sacred tool to help men, the two-legged, walk this earth. She elucidated the pipe's symbolism, explaining that the earth is our mother and grandmother. The bowl of the pipe is made of red stone, also called pipestone, which represents the earth. Carved in the stone and facing the center is a buffalo calf that represents all the four-legged creatures. The stem of the pipe is made of wood, which represents all living things on this earth. The twelve feathers that hang from where the stem meets the bowl represent the spotted eagle and all the winged creatures. All people and all things of the universe are joined, because when you pray with this pipe, you pray for and with everything.

After giving elaborate instructions on the proper use of the sacred pipe, she reminded the people that it will take them to the end of time. She further advised them that in her were four ages and that she would look after them in each age and return in the end. As she left, she miraculously transformed into a red and brown buffalo calf. She walked farther and was transformed into a white buffalo. As she contin-

ued to walk, she turned into a black buffalo.

According to Sioux mythology, in the beginning, the buffalo (properly the American bison) was placed at the West to hold back the waters. Each of the buffalo's four legs represent an age or era in the cycle of spirituality. During the course of these four ages (or eras), spirituality is gradually obscured until catastrophe hits and the cycle begins again. Every year the buffalo loses one hair, and with every age the buffalo loses one leg. The Sioux prophecy is strikingly similar to that of the Hindus. They believe that the buffalo today stands on his last leg and has become very nearly bald.

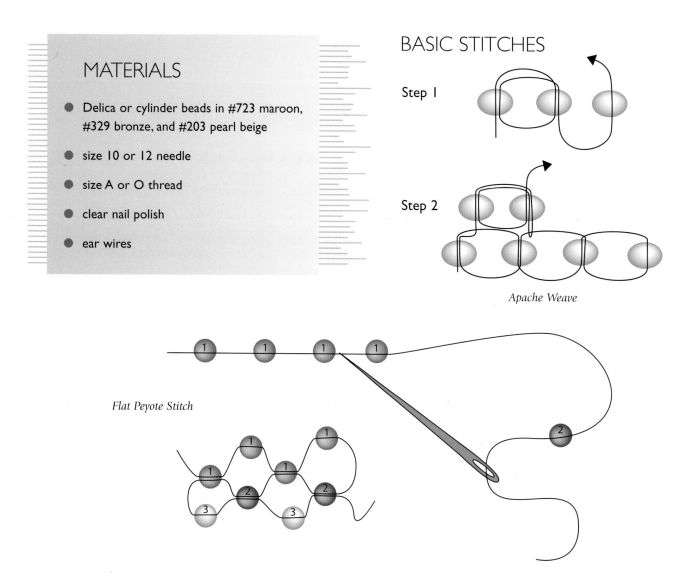

MATERIALS

- Delica or cylinder beads in #723 maroon, #329 bronze, and #203 pearl beige

- size 10 or 12 needle

- size A or O thread

- clear nail polish

- ear wires

BASIC STITCHES

Step 1

Step 2

Apache Weave

Flat Peyote Stitch

Project Notes This project uses Apache weave. It's also called brick stitch, stacking stitch, Comanche weave, or Cheyenne stitch, in case you're more familiar with those names. The bead rows stack on top of one another like a brick wall. It is a two-dimensional weave, but there's also a three-dimensional version of the stitch. Apache weave is a useful stitch for making earrings as well as beaded pieces for decorating clothing or leather. The project actually includes two patterns of a white buffalo on a pottery design. Either pattern can be used for earrings with or without fringe. The bead pieces can also be used as components in elaborate jewelry design, like necklace straps or bead strips for clothing.

Flat peyote stitch is used to bead the base of the earring. Some beaders are accustomed to using ladder stitch; either technique is acceptable.

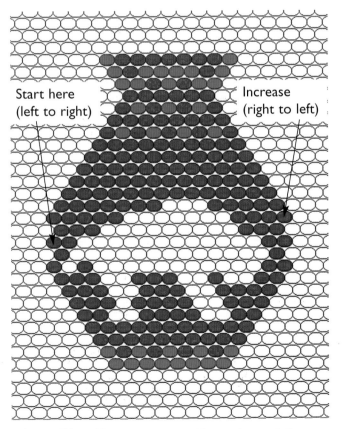

White Buffalo Calf Pattern 1 Designed by Jonathan M. Pulley

1. Begin by placing 3 beads on your needle and thread, following the pattern shown. Run your needle through the bottom of the first bead to form a triangle. Tie a square knot to secure and seal with clear nail polish.

2. We will bead the base with a 2-bead row of flat peyote stitch. The arrow on the pattern at left marks where you start. (See the introduction for how to read an Apache weave or brick-stitch pattern.) Some beaders prefer to do the base row with a ladder stitch, but this method is more stable and secure. Pick up one bead and pass your needle through the bead at the bottom of the triangle. Continue adding beads until you complete the first two rows.

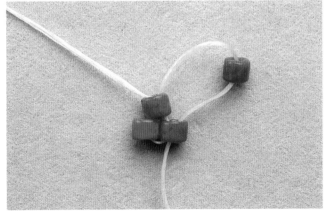

3. The next row involves an increase, which simply means that you add 2 beads and pass your needle under the first thread bridge. Secure the beads by passing the needle up the closest bead added, down the second bead added, and back up the first bead. I call this the "up-down-up thing." See Apache weave step 2.

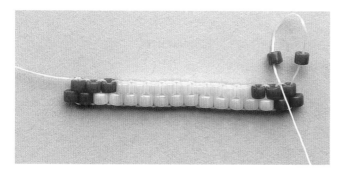

4. The rest of the row is finished by adding only one bead at a time.

5. When you have completed the top half of the design, add a 6-bead loop in the center and place the ear wire in the middle of it. Reinforce by passing your needle and thread through the loop at least two times. Weave your needle down to the base row, turn your beadwork upside down, and finish the bottom half of the design. Begin your fringe by having your needle exit the last bead

in the row. Add beads according to the picture at the selected length. You do the turnaround by skipping over the last 3 beads on your thread and running your needle back though the fringe beads and the base-row bead.

6. Continue adding fringe according to your creative design and length. Here are the finished white buffalo calf earrings with and without fringe.

VARIATIONS

The White Buffalo Calf Pattern 2 shows a variation that can be made into the gold-colored earrings shown, with or without fringe.

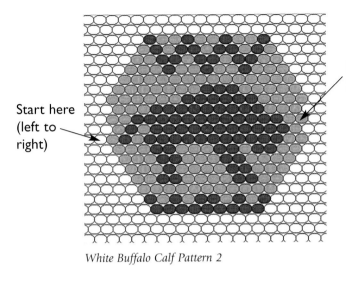

Increase
(right to left)

Start here
(left to
right)

White Buffalo Calf Pattern 2

The medicine bag at right shows how beadwork can be applied to leather for embellishment. Attach it very carefully with supple leather glue and sew it on with a needle and thread using small, discrete stitches. Find the pattern for the medicine bag on page 118.

4

Sun-Rosette Medallion

APPLIQUÉ AND FRETTING STITCH

INTERMEDIATE

The sun is the physical manifestation of Wakan Tanka (God), giver of life and light. The sun has been used by humankind through the ages as a symbol of life and regeneration. The heat and light from the sun are absolutely necessary for human survival as well as to the survival of other animals and plants.

The sun rosette used in this project was fashioned after an ancient symbol carved into a rock in the South Mountains in Phoenix, Arizona. It is a simple image with profound significance. The image was translated into a bead design by stitching beads in concentric circles.

The Sun Dance, a major communal ceremony celebrated by many Native tribes, was most notably associated with the Plains Indians. This spiritual ceremony emphasizes renewal through the element of sacrifice on the part of its participants. Human beings, like other animals, must all cooperate in order to ensure universal regeneration. Prominent animal symbols include the buffalo and the eagle. The dancers undergo a certain amount of pain in order to achieve spiritual transcendence, breaking loose from the bonds of ignorance.

This brief summary cannot explain the profound significance of the Sun Dance. Like any spiritual activity, personal exploration and involvement are necessary to comprehend and experience enlightenment. For more insight, read the revealing book by Leonard Peltier, Prison Writings: My Life Is My Sun Dance. *Peltier is a well-known political prisoner and modern-day spiritual warrior. He epitomizes the concept of sacrifice, which makes him a hero for many and feared by others.*

MATERIALS

- 4 x 4-inch square of adhesive-backed felt (Sticky-Back felt), Ultrasuede, or thin leather

- 4 x 4-inch square of leather or other backing material

- size 11 seed beads, two or three colors

- size 10 or 12 beading needle

- size A or O beading thread

- fabric or leather glue

- scissors

- single-edge razor blade

- liquid fabric stiffener or stiff backing like cardboard, card stock paper, or thin plastic

BASIC STITCHES

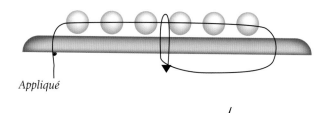

Appliqué

Step 1
Pick up 3 beads.

Step 2
Pick up 2 beads.

Fretting Stitch

Project Notes

Historically, this sun medallion or shield has been referred to as a rosette, which is beaded in concentric circles and often worn as part of dance regalia. The term *appliqué* refers to a sewing technique in which beads are applied to fabric. The term *couching,* or backstitching, is used to describe the method of tacking down beads with thread. The pendant can be hung from a beaded rope in a more contemporary fashion. The instructions for the circular netting rope are included in Chapter 10.

Use fabric or leather glue; hard epoxy glues or stiff cements are not recommended.

1. Cut out a small square window from the center of the paper backing on the 4 x 4-inch adhesive-backed felt with a single-edge razor or X-acto knife. Peel off the small white paper square and leave the remaining white-paper frame. The adhesive-backed felt holds your beads temporarily in place until they are tacked down. Work with the adhesive side of the felt facing you.

2. Thread your needle with about a yard of thread and tie a knot in one of the thread ends. Run your needle from back to front so that the needle comes out in the center of the fabric square. Pick up one bead and tack it down by running your needle from front to back (the "wrong side" of the work).

3. Move your needle to the front by coming up right next to the first bead. Pick up 4 beads and place them around the first bead as shown. Tack down the threads between each bead, with your needle coming out of the last bead.

4. Pick up 3 more beads to complete the circle and tack down between each bead.

5. Moving your needle over about one bead wide, pick up 4 to 6 beads. You will be tacking down the last bead and then moving your needle to tack down the thread in the middle. If you pick up 6 beads, you will tack down between the third and fourth bead to stabilize the row.

Review the appliqué drawing on page 32.

Then, tack down each bead that you just added except the last one. Your needle should come out of the last bead added. Be careful with your tension because if it is too tight, your rosette will be concave instead of flat. It is better to have a relaxed tension so that the beads have slight gaps rather than being too crowded. When you have completed your design, you can tighten up the beadwork by running your needle and thread through the last row of beads and pulling gently.

6. When you have completed your beadwork design, cut out the beadwork with sharp scissors placed parallel to the beads, leaving a slight edge. (Be careful not to cut through any threads securing the beads to the felt.) Trace around the beadwork on your backing material and cut it out. Liquid fabric stiffener is recommended for larger pieces of beadwork but not required for small earrings. Other types of stiff backing (see materials) can be sandwiched between the beadwork and the backing. Glue the backing to the beadwork, being careful that the glue does not bleed into the beads. Do not apply glue all the way to the edge, leaving at least ⅛ inch so that the glue doesn't interfere with your beaded edging.

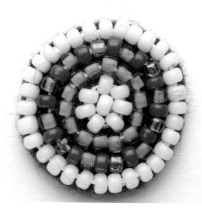

Steps 5 and 6 show how the beadwork is cut out, and the order in which it is layered to include the beadwork, backing, and jewelry hardware. In this case, a flat-pad post earring back

is shown, but the medallion only requires fabric stiffener and Ultrasuede or leather backing.

7. Sew a beaded edge, called fretting, to your earrings or medallion. (See the fretting stitch on page 32.) Below right is a sun medallion with fringe.

8. Add fringe in any length that looks appealing. Add a beaded strap or attach a neck strap with stiff stringing wire or artificial sinew. The necklace must be very sturdy to endure a lot of movement, especially if the rosette is to be worn by a dancer. The beaded strap shown

on page 35 is done with circular netting; find instructions in Chapter 10. The matching earrings are much less time-consuming to bead.

9. Using the photo of the beadwork as a pattern, make your beadwork piece larger by adding rows, as shown on page opposite.

10. The pendant can be used with a pin back, tied onto hair or clothing with leather lace, or suspended with some type of necklace chain or rope. See instructions for circular netting rope in Chapter 10. The finishing ends vary slightly depending on whether the rope is used as a necklace, amulet-bag strap, or eyeglass holder.

VARIATIONS

The earrings below, made by Genny Hatathlie, are a fine example of appliqué-stitch done with size 13 Charlotte-cut beads.

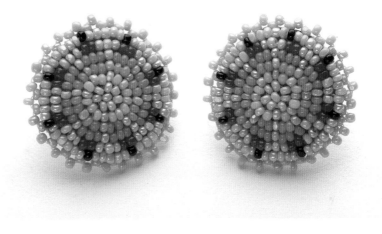

Sylvia Elam made these extravagant multicolored gemstone cabochon earrings.

5 Zuni Triple-Strand Bracelet

STRINGING

BEGINNER

This Zuni triple-strand bracelet is named after a Pueblo tribe not known for its beadwork. Historically, they have adapted their artwork to reflect styles more commonly affiliated with other tribes, such as Navajo silverwork and Pueblo pottery. The interesting point is that an artist can be influenced by many factors, including physical surroundings, cultural education or tradition, and availability of materials for a specific art form. It is not uncommon for an artist to become an apprentice with a different tribe in order to learn a specific art form. Turquoise, silver, onyx, coral, and shell are among materials that both artists and buyers seek. These materials can be used in stringing projects, silverwork, fetishes, inlay work, and even pottery. Modern artists are limited in the art form only by their imagination. Few Native artists feel limited by tribal affiliation or reputation.

Beadwork has become a notable addition to the exquisite art production of many tribes, including the Zuni. It is a notable item in the tourist trade, often displacing pottery and silversmithing. This simple project highlights the fact that Zuni beadwork is some of the most complicated and exquisite on the market today. Whether the beadwork is a stringing project of heishe, bone, shell, fetishes, or glass beads, its outstanding beauty emanates.

- 6-mm glass or metal bead for ball clasp
- glass seed beads, one color
- assorted gem chips
- chunky accent beads
- bugle beads, one color
- size 10 beading needle
- size O or B thread or Silamide
- beeswax

Project Notes This simple triple-strand bracelet mixes glass seed beads and gem chips of turquoise, goldstone, coral, and amber. The technique of using a functional beaded ball-and-loop clasp dispels the need for any hardware. Directions here are for making a bracelet, but you can create a necklace by merely increasing its length.

This chapter features a simple bracelet, but a creative beader can see that the technique of stringing multiple strands together can be quite versatile and work well for many different projects. For example, it is easily adapted to make an amulet-bag strap or a necklace. When more than one strand of beads is used, durability increases. Similar to braiding, this multiple-strand technique helps strengthens individual bead strands and allows them to safely hold a heavy pendant or gemstones.

The gemstone chips featured here are somewhat heavy and typically could not be accommodated by stringing with ordinary beading thread. The weight of the gemstones would make the thread sag or break. Heavier threads or cord might not be able to accommodate the smaller seed beads. However, when used with the technique of weaving multiple strands together, the resulting beadwork is safe, secure, and attractive.

When selecting your beads, check to make sure that the chips you use are not sharp or broken on the edges. If they are sharp, they could slice your thread. Since gemstone chips are not all the same size, the size of the bead is not as critical as the size of the hole. You may need to substitute a heavier or waxed cord if your beads are larger than the ones pictured here.

The ball-and-loop clasp is also versatile for any type of jewelry requiring a clasp, such as a choker. Any large-holed bead can be covered with beads to create a beaded bead as part of a clasp or used separately as an accent bead. A bracelet made entirely out of beaded beads or mixed with seed beads would be unique.

1. We will begin the project by covering a 6-mm bead with seed beads for one end of the ball clasp. Without picking up any beads, run your needle through the large 6-mm bead and then tie a square knot. Glue with clear nail polish. Do NOT trim your tail.

2. String 5 or 6 beads, as needed to fit around the large bead, and run your needle through the large bead again.

3. Continue wrapping beads in the same manner until the bead is covered. Tie a square knot with your original thread tail and glue with clear nail polish.

4. Using your existing thread, string 5 seed beads, a chunky gemstone bead (coral is shown), 5 seed beads, and a bugle bead. Repeat the pattern until you reach the approximate length of the bracelet and end with a chunky gemstone bead. Seven to 8 inches is the standard length for a bracelet, including the clasp, to fit an adult wrist.

5. Make a loop with seed beads that fits the beaded ball part of the clasp. Try it on for size and adjust the number of beads for a perfect fit. Change directions of your thread path by running your needle through the chunky gemstone bead in the opposite direction. Now add a different pattern of small beads to string through each large chunky bead along one side of the bracelet. Since gemstone beads are somewhat irregular in size, the actual count of the seed beads is not as important as the fit.

6. The second and third strand of beads, along opposite sides of the bracelet, should fit snugly with no thread showing. The

second and third strands of beads will be added from coral bead to coral bead. The pattern shown at bottom left consists of 3 seed beads, a small amber chip, 3 seed beads, a small gold-stone chip, 3 seed beads, a small amber chip, and 3 seed beads.

7. Continue adding sections of beads until you reach the beaded ball. Turn around by running your needle through the center of the beaded ball and adding a small turquoise chip. Skip over the turquoise chip and go back through the inside of the beaded ball.

8. Using the same thread, add your third row by stringing 7 seed beads, a small turquoise chip, and 7 seed beads from one coral bead to the next. When you are finished, tie off with an in-line knot (also called a half-hitch knot) and glue with clear nail polish. After the nail polish dries, trim your tail with scissors.

VARIATION

The necklace below is a variation on the design. The clasp is worn in front, instead of behind the neck. A little fringe added from the ball makes an interesting twist.

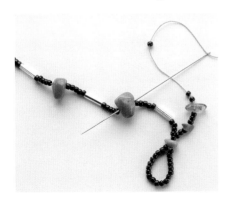

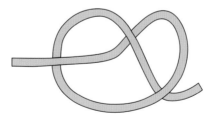

In-line Knot

Horsehair Hatband

EVEN-COUNT ROUND PEYOTE STITCH AND FLAT PEYOTE STITCH

ADVANCED

*H*orses are strong, swift, and agile animals that have contributed tremendously to the lifestyle of Native American peoples who have lived for centuries on the North American continent. While Spanish explorers have been credited with bringing horses to the New World in the sixteenth century, some evidence suggests that horses existed in North American long before Europeans arrived.

Horsehair appears in Native arts and crafts as a tribute to the animal that has influenced so many details of daily life. Travel on horseback brought greater freedom and greater mobility to a nomadic people. This beast of burden carried not only children and adults but many heavy household belongings as well.

Historians describe the sixteenth century arrival of the Spanish Conquistadors as a violent period of cruel bloodshed and severe religious and cultural intolerance. The Conquistadors and those who followed attempted to conquer and convert as well as to claim their fortunes in gold and to rape the wealth of the New World. Showing up with horses and guns, these newcomers were no doubt perceived by Native peoples much as we would international terrorists today.

Spaniards claimed lands in the Americas which they called New Spain. Much of what is now the Southwest United States, from Texas to California, was invaded by the others who caused destruction and massive cultural changes. Although Native peoples were initially overpowered or weakened by European diseases, they quickly learned how to use guns and horses to gain advantage. Some tribes affected were the Azteca, Tewa, Pueblo, Apache, Hopi, Navajo, Yaqui, and Mayo of the Southwest U.S. and south of the present-day U.S. border.

Fortunately, horses are more often recognized in modern society as a status symbol or sign of wealth than as an instrument of war or transportation. Since 1925, the city of Tucson has boasted the largest nonmotorized parade in the country, including horse-drawn coaches, real cowboys, and real Indians. Cultural artifacts and memorabilia of the Old West are an interesting reminder that the world was a radically different place less than a century ago.

MATERIALS

- horsehair (from a craft store, trading post, or horse owner)

- ½-inch cord, rope, or fabric trim, about 32 inches long (length depends on hat size)

- seed beads (any consistent size will work)

- size A or O beading thread

- size 10 or 12 beading needle

- scraps of leather or synthetic Ultrasuede

- leather or fabric glue

- transparent tape

BASIC STITCHES

Step 1

Step 2

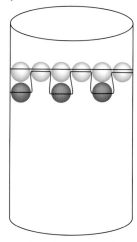

Round Peyote Stitch

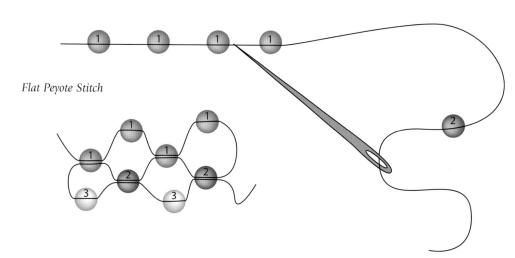

Flat Peyote Stitch

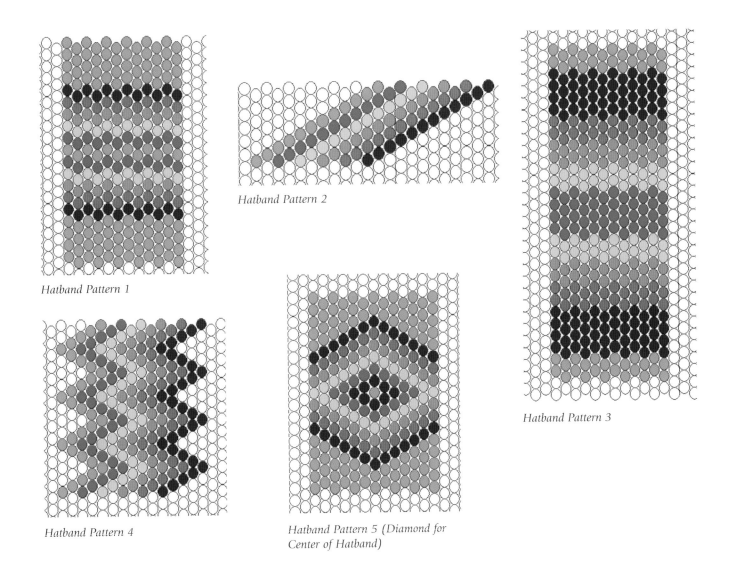

Hatband Pattern 1

Hatband Pattern 2

Hatband Pattern 3

Hatband Pattern 4

Hatband Pattern 5 (Diamond for Center of Hatband)

Project Notes You'll notice that we've included five different patterns for the hatband. The diamond pattern will be in the center of the completed hatband (see the photo on page 40), and the first half of the hatband repeats in the second half. Any of these patterns can be used as a repeating pattern for the entire length of the hatband. Choose the one or ones that suit your taste.

Wrap a piece of clear adhesive tape around the ends of your cord to prevent unraveling. Although this project uses an even-count peyote stitch, an advanced beader can easily learn odd-count peyote, which spirals instead of having discrete rows with a beginning and end. It is easier for the inexperienced beader to follow a pattern with even-count rather than odd-count peyote stitch.

The finished hatband in this project uses all five patterns in this order: 1, 2, 3, 4, 5, 4, 3, 2, 1. However, you can use any or all of the patterns in any order to create your own distinctive hatband. I've used the diamond pattern (pattern 5) in the middle of the hatband shown here.

You'll be using even-count round peyote stitch and flat peyote stitch.

1. Tie a ring of beads around your cord with a square knot, being careful to use an even number.

3. At the end of the first row, you will "drop down" by passing your needle through the first bead added from the previous row.

the end of the first row, tie your two thread ends into a square knot to stabilize your beads.

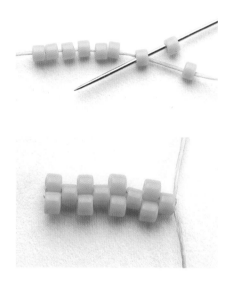

2. Using Hatband Pattern 1, thread one bead onto the needle, skip a bead, and run your needle through the following bead. If your first row has 12 beads, your second row will have 6 beads, since you are adding only every other bead.

4. Continue adding beads the same way, closely following the pattern for color changes. Try to keep a somewhat relaxed tension so that your rope remains fluid rather than stiff.

5. Periodically, try your hatband on for size or measure the circumference of the hatband to determine the finished length necessary to fit your hat. To make the slide, which allows the hatband to be adjustable, string 8 beads on your thread. Use a stop bead, if necessary, to prevent your beads from falling off.

6. Pick up one bead, skip a bead, and pass the needle through the next bead, as shown. This is called flat peyote stitch. At

7. After you have added enough rows of beads to form a ring which fits around both cord ends, you are ready to zipper stitch the two ends to make a continuous ring. With your needle and thread, zigzag from one side to the other to attach the beads that stick out. You will notice that they fit just like a zipper.

8. When you have completed the slide, insert the ends of the hatband through the completed slide in opposite directions so that the ends cross in the middle of the slide. Now you are ready to finish the ends with horsehair and beadwork.

9. Get a small bundle of horsehair and fold it in half. Put the cord end in the middle of the horsehair and bind them together tightly with thread. Cut a small piece of leather or Ultrasuede to fit evenly around the cord. Spread leather glue on the fabric and wrap snugly around the end, being careful not to overlap the seams. Stitch with thread to hold the seam securely in place.

10. Using round peyote stitch, bead tightly around the leather to secure one end. Repeat on the other end of the hatband.

Use of horsehair in such things as braids, key rings, pottery, baskets, and beadwork is often a very personal tribute to a horse by its owner, who recognizes it as a magnificent and beautiful creature.

The stylized drawing of a horse (shown below) is my personal business logo, designed by Gerald Dawavendewa, an internationally recognized Hopi artist.

VARIATION

Here is a style of loomed hatband. It's more commonly seen and less expensive than the beaded hatband created with the peyote stitch featured in this chapter.

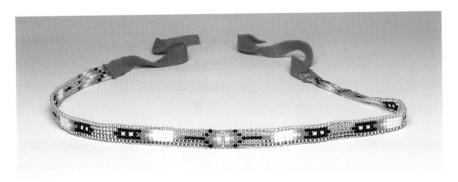

7 Coyote Pottery Earrings

The coyote is a tenacious creature, known by many names. The word coyote *originates from the Aztec* coyotl, *commonly known as a barking dog or little wolf. The scientific name is* Canis latrans. *He is also referred to as Ki-o-ti, the most influential of all the animal people. Regardless of the many different human attitudes toward this creature, basic facts about the coyote are fascinating.*

He is found throughout the United States and Canada, making him quite adaptable to varying climates and environments. Known as a relative of the wolf, the coyote does interbreed with domestic dogs, but this is somewhat rare because of their different breeding cycles. The population of coyotes continues to flourish in North America. The coyote is a carnivore, but he also eats many fruits and nuts as well as birds and small rodents. Coyotes play an essential role in the balance of nature by keeping the populations of pack rats, field mice, and ground squirrels under control.

Many stories are told about the coyote and his interesting personality, which are projections of human traits into animal behavior. He is known as sly, cunning, and a trickster. He is somewhat shy of humans, probably because coyotes are often considered vermin and targeted by people for mass slaughter. Although they have been observed to prey on cattle and sheep, they frequently feast on carrion after the animal has met its demise in some other fashion.

Many different tribes have stories where the coyote is an animal, but he is often a man, a very handsome and charming young man. I have had the pleasure of knowing and raising a delightful coydog (half-dog and half-coyote), who does indeed live up to the image and reputation of many coyote tales.

The pattern used for this project was fashioned after our coydog Gibson, who has the classic features of an icon. He looks like a black coyote. His mother was a Rottweiler and his father a handsome coyote. While living on the outskirts of Tucson, a male coyote unlatched our wrought-iron gate to court our family dog, Zuni. After having fun taking care of their eight puppies, my son decided to keep the littlest one because of his delightful personality.

Forever burned in my memory is the sight of Gibson whimpering and howling after his last sibling was adopted. He looked like a classic howling coyote icon. He has joined our human clan and has become socialized in many ways. His wild nature, curiosity, playfulness, and survivability are quite entertaining and educational. He loves to snack on bugs, gourd seeds, and oranges. He also likes to eat my peppermint and sunflower plants. He is also loyal and very affectionate, enjoying a good group hug whenever we have family gatherings.

MATERIALS

- seed beads, Delicas, or hex beads in your favorite size and color

- size 10 or 12 beading needle

- size A or O beading needle

- pair of ear wires

BASIC STITCHES

Step 1

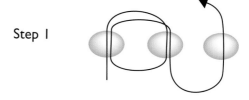

Step 2

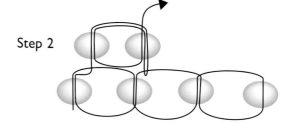

Apache Weave

Flat Peyote Stitch

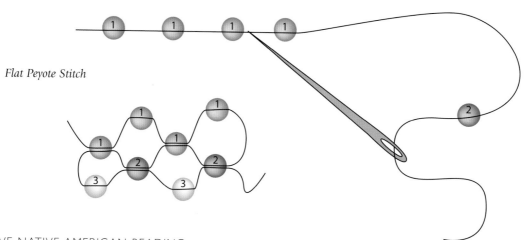

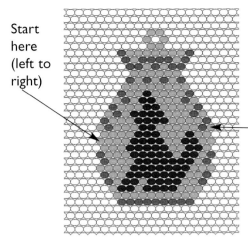

Start here (left to right)

Increase row (right to left)

Coyote Pottery Pattern

Project Notes

The pottery shape is created with a technique called Apache weave. It is also called stacking stitch, increasing brick stitch, or Comanche weave. The base row is made with flat peyote stitch. The image of the howling coyote is embedded within the outer shape of a vase or pottery vessel. The finished beadwork makes darling earrings or jewelry components. The coyote pattern was designed by Jonathan M. Pulley.

We've used #421 copper, #322 brown, and #10 black seed beads for this project. You can use Delicas or hex beads and choose your favorite size and colors.

1. Begin at the arrow shown on the pattern.

2. Put 3 beads on your needle and go back through the first bead as shown. Tie a square knot in your thread.

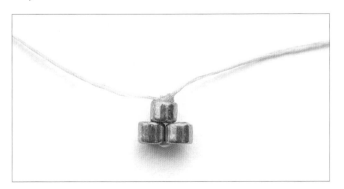

3. You will be making the base by making a 2-bead row of flat peyote stitch. The pattern shows you where to start as indicated by an arrow. (Review the section in the Intrtoduction about how to read a beading pattern.)

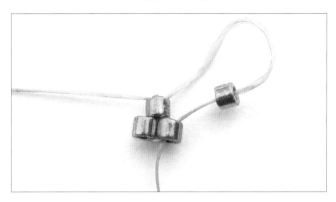

4. To increase, you will need to pick up two beads and pass your needle under the first thread bridge.

5. Pass your needle up the second bead, down the first bead, and back up the second bead. I call this the "up-down-up thing." See Apache weave step 2.

6. Continue the row by adding only one bead at a time, passing your needle under the thread bridge and back through the bead you just added. This stitch automatically decreases by one bead each row, unless you increase.

7. When you have reached the top of the earring, add the 6-bead loop and enclose the ear wire. Reinforce the loop with at least two passes of thread and then weave your thread back down to the base row. Turn your work upside down and complete the bottom half of the pattern.

These earrings look good either with or without fringe. Be creative and make a matching bracelet, necklace, or amulet bag.

8

Free-Form Peyote Bracelet

FLAT PEYOTE STITCH

INTERMEDIATE

*H*istorically, peyote stitch has been one of the most popular beading techniques credited to Native American beadwork. It is a wonderful and utilitarian stitch. This chapter features a derivative of that stitch which is quite creative and versatile as well.

Beading novices often see the free-form peyote stitch as impossible and chaotic. This stitch seems to be liberating for creative folks who like challenges and freedom but very frustrating for those who prefer structure. As a retired psychologist, it has been amusing for me to assess various personality types when I hear each person's judgment about the technique. It's fun for those who like to explore outside the boundaries and create three-dimensionally. As I explain to my beading students, the world we live in is not two-dimensional. By exploring the third dimension, you may find that it can become quite natural and comfortable.

This bracelet project does give some basic structure to the free-form technique, but we encourage your creativity. Like nature, the bracelet will not be perfectly symmetrical, but the piece is quite balanced and comfortable to wear. Although we're making a bracelet here, the technique is useful for creating bead fabric and many different objects of beauty.

MATERIALS

- seed beads, five or six different sizes and colors
- assorted fancy embellishment beads
- size B waxed thread
- size 10 beading needle
- large bead or button for clasp

BASIC STITCHES

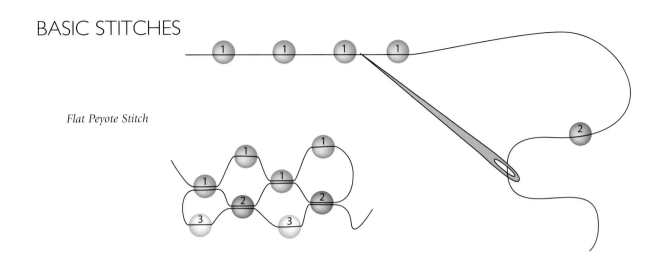

Flat Peyote Stitch

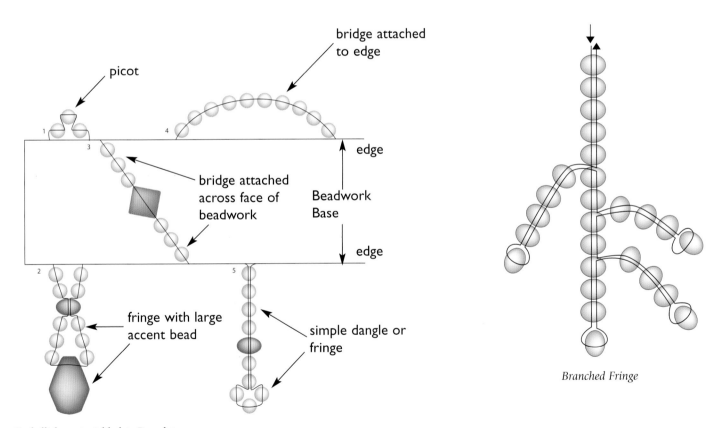

Embellishments Added to Bracelet

Branched Fringe

Project Notes We will begin with a strand of assorted beads about 8 inches long. The average bracelet length is 7½ to 8 inches long, including the clasp. Knowledge of flat peyote stitch is helpful but not necessary. Since the beaded piece tends to twist and turn a bit, it will end up being a little shorter than the original length. We will bead about five to six rows as a base before we begin creating thread bridges, loops, fringe, and embellishment. In general, I recommend that you string sections of 6 to 8 beads of the same size before adding another section of 6 to 8 beads of a different size. Be careful not to add too many large beads next to each other because the weight will make the beadwork unstable. It is better to use the larger beads for embellishing the base row.

The first time you try this technique, I advise that you use two complementary or contrasting colors of all beads (like black and white) or a monochromatic theme, such as several different shades of one color. For instance, you could use light blue, medium blue, and dark blue.

For embellishment beads, you could use triangles, cubes, flowers, leaves, teardrops, fire-polish beads, gemstone chips, fetishes, or pearls. Also see the drawings for several ways to embellish the bracelet with various picots, bridges, fringes, or dangles.

1. String sections of different seed beads, as shown for a total length of about 8 inches, adding an occasional accent bead.

2. Using flat peyote stitch, add one bead every other bead, using the same size beads in each section. (For beginners, pick up one bead, skip a bead, and pass your needle through the next bead.) When you get to a larger accent bead, pass the needle through that bead and continue adding one bead every other bead. When you get to the end, continue beading down the other side, being careful not to pass your needle through the same bead more than two to three times. Keep your thread taut so that no thread is showing.

3. When you get to a good spot, add a bridge by stringing a set of beads from one point on the bracelet to another.

4. Continue adding beads with flat peyote stitch or embellishment on one side of the base and then the other, being careful not to crowd the beads at the end by passing the thread too many times through the same bead. Experiment with weaving in and out of the base to get to the spot where you need to add another accent bead. Add embellishment beads throughout the face of the bracelet to create an appealing and well-balanced piece of art.

See the drawings on page 53 to give you an idea of various embellishment techniques (picots, bridges, fringes, or dangles, and branched fringe). The possibilities are limited only by your beads and findings. If the bead or accent piece(s) has a hole, it can be attached to another bead.

Just be careful not to let your thread show, but make sure the thread passes through a bead hole. Do not add beads from the front of the piece to the back as you would if you were sewing on a button. Your thread should pass through a bead hole so that there is no thread showing from the front or the back.

5. When you are finished with the beading, add a conventional clasp or use a larger bead or button. Add a loop of beads that fits snugly over the bead or button clasp. Attach the loop securely since the bracelet will carry some weight and have to endure some wear.

VARIATION

Here's a black and red bracelet that shows a variation. When you're comfortable with this liberating technique, try making earrings, a pendant, or even a wall hanging. Your imagination is the only limiting factor with free-form peyote stitch.

9

Blue Violet Flower

Native Americans are recognized worldwide for their knowledge regarding medicinal plants. Their spiritual philosophy of keeping in balance with all of creation does more that just give lip service to serious environmental issues facing the world today. They were the original environmentalists. Their methods of hunting and farming and their lifestyle in general show their understanding and sensitivity toward all living things.

Many plants are known to contain powerful medicinal qualities that can help humankind enjoy more comfortable lives, free of sickness and disease. Knowledge about medicinal plants throughout the world was traditionally held by key individuals who were sacred keepers of the knowledge and who ensured that the information would be passed on to future generations. On a large scale, today we rely on medical schools, pharmaceutical companies, chemists, books, universities, and other sources of information, such as the Internet. On a small community basis, we rely on doctors, nurses, mothers, grandmothers, as well as local Native healers and health practitioners.

Virtually all medicine has been derived from an original plant source. On the local level, it is important that health practitioners are able to secure their medicine from a reliable source and, if possible, to obtain the plant in its natural state. Observation of plants growing in their natural environment or in cultivated plots is the best way to learn to identify what a plant looks like and to study its usefulness as medicine. Most people who have culinary or medicinal herbs growing in kitchen or outdoor gardens do not usually have an arsenal of chemists and pharmacists to analyze their plants and authenticate their usage. They learn from books, plant nurseries, mothers, grandmothers, and others who help them identify useful plants. One primary form of identification is the flower produced by a given plant.

The blue violet has leaves and flowers that are useful, edible, and medicinal. Many people are unaware of the violet's ethno-botanical (medicinal, folkloric, and nutritional) uses by Native Americans. The official Latin genus name is *Viola* and the plant is frequently called the common violet, not to be confused with the African violet. The flower is very sweet-smelling, and some varieties have heart-shaped leaves, which aids identification. This healing plant is not found in the Southwest desert, but a dear Apache friend introduced me to it when I was very sick with viral pneumonia.

Native tribes ranging from Canada to upstate New York, and from southern California to Georgia use different species of *Viola* for the same purpose. It is not uncommon for many tribes to trade goods among themselves. The blue-violet plant has been used for a variety of respiratory illnesses because it helps rid the body of congestion. It also contains the glycoside of salicylic acid, which substantiates its use for centuries as a pain remedy and as a sedative. The fresh flowers are used in salads and jelly, and they're candied for a decorative garnish on desserts. Originally native to Europe, it was a burial custom in Greece to cover the dead person with violets as a symbol of the beauty and the transitory quality of life. A multitude of plants in North America includes both indigenous and introduced species of violets.

This project creates a beaded blue violet that is a three-dimensional flower. You can apply the flower to baskets, jewelry, pottery, or clothing. This beautiful little flower can embellish an assortment of items like pencil tops, hair clips, napkin holders, clothing, and even ceramic pots for your herbs.

MATERIALS

- size 11 beads for the leaf in one or two shades of green (leaf beads)

- size 13, 14, or 15 beads in violet, blue violet, and yellow (flower beads)

- size 12 beading needle

- size A or O beading thread

- clear nail polish

Project Notes The pattern in this project is for the three-dimensional flower only. The leaf pattern is exactly the same as the flower pattern except that the leaf uses bigger beads. For the advanced beader, it is very easy to make the leaf first with beads at least one size bigger and then to sew the flower layer right on top of the leaf. You'll note that the flower beads are smaller than the leaf beads, so there's plenty of room to makes several passes of thread through the leaf base to attach your flower. When you're finished, use your existing thread to attach your flower to a bag, bracelet, clothing, or anywhere you would like some floral embellishment.

The photos show right-to-left or counterclockwise orientation. If you are left-handed and prefer to bead from left to right, choose the direction that feels the most comfortable, but be consistent.

I. Begin by threading your needle with about 2 yards of thread. Pick up 5 flower beads and tie them in a ring with a square knot. Glue with clear nail polish. To make it easier to see, we will use bright yellow beads at the base, although they can also be the same color as your flower or even green.

2. Add a flower bead between each bead in the ring by picking up a bead and then running the needle through the next bead of the ring. If you use two different shades of flower beads, it will be easier to discriminate which row you are on. You will notice that the beads on this row will stick out, so we'll call these pop-up beads.

3. To begin the petal, move your thread so that it comes out of a pop-up bead. Add 7 flower beads. Make your "turnaround" by skipping the seventh bead and running your needle through the sixth bead.

4. Add one bead every other bead until you get to the bottom, for a total of 3 beads. The last bead will be added by running your needle through the bottom of the petal, which is the first bead of the original 7-bead strung. This step will turn your thread path so that it is going up the right side of the petal.

5. Add one bead every other bead between the pop-up beads on the petal. Go up one side and down the other for a total of 6 beads. The photo shows the beads being added on the right side first, with the needle passing through the top bead and then down the left side. When you make your turnaround at the bottom, pass your needle through 2 beads on the right side of the petal.

6. Add 1 bead between the pop-up beads, then add 2 beads, passing your needle through the 3 top beads, add 2 beads, and then add 1 bead. When you are ready to do your turnaround, pass your needle through 3 side beads.

7. Add 2 beads, pass your needle through 7 beads around the top of the petal, and then add 2 more beads.

8. Pass your needle all the way around the edge of the petal and tighten gently to shape your petal.

9. Pass your needle through the second pop-up bead from the original ring of 5 beads to stabilize your first petal.

10. Continue beading petals until you have five petals.

11. If you choose, add 3 to 5 yellow seed beads or a 3-mm fire polish bead (depending on what size beads are used in the petals) from one side of the ring to the other for the flower center.

USES FOR THE VIOLET

Here the three-dimensional flower appears on a beaded ceramic pot, a beaded amulet bag, and a leather amulet bag.

10

Rope Eyeglass Holder

While beaders around the world make ropes of beadwork that they wrap around cotton or nylon cord or rope, Native American beaders usually prefer the peyote stitch for their beaded ropes. Square stitch, spiral stitch, and Ndebele or herringbone stitches are also commonly used to make bead ropes. This rope eyeglass holder, created with circular netting, offers a functional and attractive way to safely secure eyeglasses.

Circular netting, an interesting three-dimensional beadwork technique, can be used in a variety of jewelry pieces and as a strap for leather bags, purses, and bracelets. The center is hollow, but with tight thread tension; it serves as a very sturdy rope. The sun-rosette medallion in Chapter 4 also uses this rope or strap in the necklace.

The origin of circular netting is not clear, but the stitch has become increasingly popular with beaders who have come to appreciate its usefulness and beauty as a sturdy bead rope with many possibilities for beadwork designs. The netted rope is very supple and flexible but sturdy enough for carrying some weight. Its multidimensionality adds intrigue to the beadwork aside from the designs that add color and movement.

Although Native Americans are best known for their uses of peyote stitch, this project is often mistaken for a peyote rope because the finished appearance is similar. A solid rope of peyote stitch is time-consuming and costly because it is so labor-intensive. The beader may add only one bead at a time. However, netting adds three beads at a time, so the beadwork can be produced much more quickly and exotic designs are still possible with this stitch. Ropes are used to make lariats, long necklaces, and bolo ties.

MATERIALS

- size 11 beads, two or three colors (at least one main color and one contrast color)
- size O or B beading thread
- beeswax
- size 10 or 12 beading needle
- clear nail polish
- pair of eyeglass-holder findings

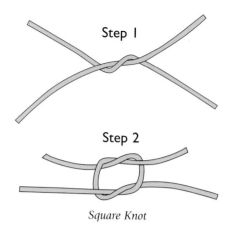

Square Knot

Project Notes This circular netting requires a bit of practice to be comfortable with holding the beadwork to achieve the proper tension. You'll be beading the project piece in midair without a base of rope or cord. However, for beginners, it's acceptable to bead around a cord if that makes it easier to learn the technique. After you master the basic technique, I recommend that you attempt to make the project without a cord so that you'll achieve the best tension. Waxed bead thread might also be helpful. Another hint: While picking beads to add in the next steps, wrap the beading thread around the index finger of the hand that's holding onto the beadwork.

The first three photos show flat beadwork, but as soon as you reach step 4, the beadwork will begin to curve, forming a hollow tube. You may notice that the first inch of your beadwork is looser than the rest of the rope. If you get frustrated, it is easy to undo the first inch so that all your beadwork will have consistent tension. Don't forget to try on the rope for a length that's comfortable for you. After all, we don't all have the same head, neck, or upper torso measurements.

The first time you try this project, use two contrasting colors of beads. After you learn the technique, you can create numerous patterns by playing with different colors and combinations for a spiral effect or color blending. For an interesting variation, you could try stringing memory wire through the bead rope after you complete it to make a sturdy and flexible bracelet or choker.

I. Begin with a ring of 6 beads. Tie a square knot and secure with clear nail polish.

2. Add 3 beads every other bead. The pattern is formed by the color of beads you select. For example, try one main color, one contrast color, and one main color. Repeat twice.

3. Add 3 beads (one main color, one contrast color, and one main color to the first contrast bead from the previous row). Repeat twice by attaching your 3 beads to the contrast or middle bead.

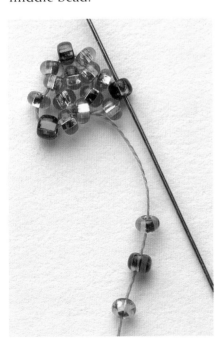

4. At this point, you will begin applying tension to make your beads start to curve. Remember that you are making a three-dimensional rope, so it will start forming a hollow tube. It helps to wrap your thread around your index finger to keep the thread tension taut as you are adding beads. You will notice that the pictures show the beads being added in a clockwise fashion when flat, but as the rope builds, it turns into a three-dimensional object. Go in whatever direction is most comfortable for you, but be consistent and do not change directions once you've started.

5. After the rope grows to the approximate length (26 inches is the average length), we will be adding a small loop at each end to enclose the eyeglass-holder finding. Reinforce the loop with thread at least twice and weave the thread into the netted rope for extra security. Tie off the thread and seal it with clear nail polish.

Thunderbird Lighter Case

ROUND PEYOTE STITCH

ADVANCED

The *mythical thunderbird design appears frequently in Native American bead-*
work. Even in modern times, many Native stories tell of a large bird that appears
on the cold front preceding violent summer thunderstorms. Some people speculate
that the thunderbird is a real bird, such a giant condor, not native to the United
States, migrating north from South America. Many sightings have been reported
of very large flying beasts that have been said to snatch small animals and even
small children.

The mythical thunderbird symbolizes an aspect of the natural world. Some have
described the thunderbird as having teeth but no head or an insignificant one. The
thunderbird is violent and destructive but also recognized as a benevolent cleans-
ing agent. Images typically show him upright with his tail feathers fanned and his
wings spread.

One Native story relates how the thunderbird came from the West, the direction
of danger. He had the power to cause thunder by flapping his wings and to make
lightning by blinking his eyes. Along with the rain comes the smell of danger
accompanied by powerful lightning bolts filling the skies. The duality of the thun-
derbird symbol is incredible. The thunderbird symbolizes day and night, destruc-
tion and rebirth, danger and safety, dry and wet, real and unreal, life and death.

A famous Kiowa poet, N. Scott Momaday, describes a different beast that roams
the sky during a thunderstorm. In his book, The Way to Rainy Mountain, *Moma-*
day's beast has a horse's head and a fish's tail. From its mouth lightning flashes, and
its tail embodies the hot wind of a tornado. During a particularly violent monsoon-
like season in southern Arizona, his description comes to life. These storms can tear
down telephone poles, uproot large trees, and rip roofs off houses. Every season peo-
ple drown because of the resulting flash flooding in previously dry washes. Animals
are displaced, millions of seeds sprout, and flowers appear on plants that had once

looked dead. An incredible transformation takes place before your very eyes. The water nourishes the parched earth and the desert miraculously comes alive.

This project is a beaded lighter case, which makes its own lightning. Although a disposable lighter is a utilitarian object, it represents fire, one of the most powerful forces of nature. Fire is a source of heat, light, and destruction, depending on how it is used. Practically speaking, fire is also used to cook food, burn incense, or light candles. The owner of a lighter possesses the power of fire at his fingertips. Having respect for this power, the owner can use the lighter for a positive rather than a negative purpose. Of course, one need not be a smoker.

MATERIALS

- metal lighter case (available from silversmith suppliers)
- fabric for covering the metal case (prefer thin leather or Ultrasuede)
- white glue or leather glue
- Delica beads, one tube each of #603 silver-lined red, #100 silver-lined orange, #10 black, #167 light blue AB, #47 silver-lined cobalt blue
- size O or A beading thread
- size 10 or 12 beading needle

BASIC STITCH

Step 1

Round Peyote Stitch

Step 2

Project Notes You can find the metal lighter case in drug stores and neighborhood markets or from silversmith suppliers. First we cover the metal case with leather, felt, Ultrasuede, or synthetic fabric, which serves as a cushion for the beads. In the thunderbird pattern, 56 beads are across and 36 beads from top to bottom. The metal case is slightly larger than the plastic lighter, which allows for the removal and replacement of the actual lighter when the fluid runs out.

The patterns in this chapter can be read from the top down or from the bottom up so that there is no arrow to indicate where to begin. (See the Introduction for how to read a beading pattern.)

You can use the thunderbird and other patterns in this chapter for other projects as well. Designed to fit a standard lighter case, the pattern can also be used to create an amulet bag. If you prefer to increase the width, simply add background beads on each side of the pattern in an equal number. To increase the overall length, add more rows at the top and the bottom or add beaded fringe or leather fringe. You can add a necklace strap using the technique described in Chapter 6, peyote rope; Chapter 2, badge holder necklace; Chapter 8, freeform peyote; Chapter 5, triple-strand bracelet; or Chapter 10, netted rope.

The same design may appear on the front and back of some of the patterns here. If you want your project to go faster, you can bead the pattern on the front and use background beads on the back. For patterns having a different design on each side, you can bead each pattern separately in flat peyote stitch and make a striking pendant for a necklace or a piece of beadwork to add to clothing or a leather bag. Of course, you can use your own color combinations on any of the patterns offered for this project. With a little creative effort, the patterns can also be used to bead onto a candle holder, a small vase, a fabric or leather creation, or even a purse.

For those who encounter social ostracism for smoking tobacco in public places, remember that lighters are also used to ignite gas-heating stoves, fireplaces, camp fires, barbeque grills, candles, and incense. Fancy lighter cases are frequently used for special occasions like ceremonies that use incense. With this thunderbird case, a fortunate family member can show off the beading skill and designs associated with the particular tribe or clan.

Round peyote stitch is also called circular peyote stitch.

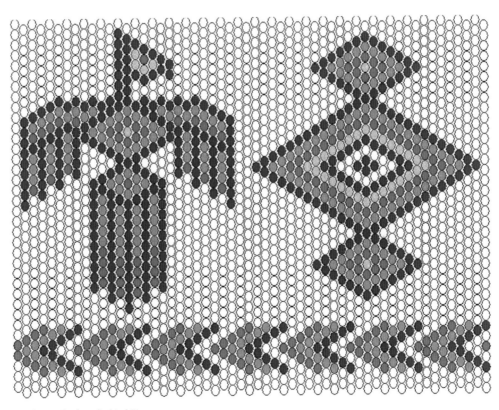

Traditional Thunderbird Pattern

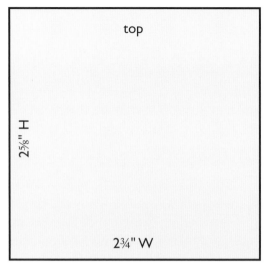

Leather Pattern

top

2⅝" H

2¾" W

2. Use glue to attach the fabric to the metal, being careful not to overlap the seams and leaving at least ⅛ inch unglued at the top so that the glue does not interfere with sewing on the beadwork. Trim as necessary.

Put about 1 yard of thread on your needle and pick up 56 beads, following the pattern.

3. Tie your beads into a ring around the metal lighter case, being careful not to cover the indentation where the lighter tab fits.

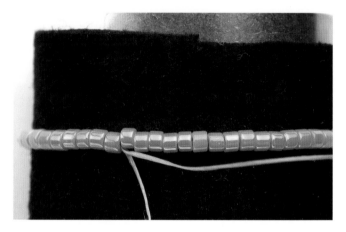

1. Using the pattern shown, cut a piece of leather or fabric to wrap around the metal lighter case.

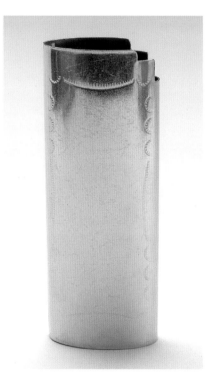

4. Follow the pattern with round peyote stitch by adding one bead every other bead until you get to the end of the row.

5. Drop down by passing your needle through the first bead of the previous row before you continue adding one bead every other bead.

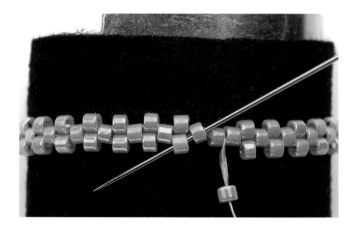

6. After your first few rows are established, slide your beadwork to the top and tack it down to the fabric edge with tiny stitches. Continue following the pattern until it is completed. Embellish with beaded fringe if you choose.

VARIATIONS

Here are patterns for other beaded lighter cases you might want to make. I've included my abstract geometric-cross pattern. Sheila Vinson has designed the other three patterns: an alternate thunderbird design, a turtle design, and the Ojo de Dios. The patterns can be easily adapted to make an amulet bag by increasing the width from 56 beads to 60 beads and adding a strap. Cylinder beads were used here, but other types and sizes of beads can be used with minor modifications in the bead count.

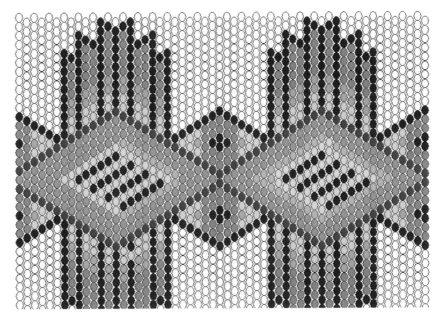

Geometric-Cross Pattern

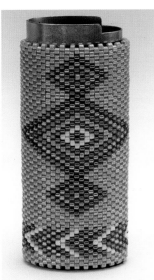

The pink lighter case with an abstract geometric-cross pattern uses Delica #200 dusty pink AB, #796 maroon, #1340 silver-lined fuchsia, #175 transparent green AB finish, and #426 metallic light green.

Sheila Vinson's turtle pattern uses Delica #732 opaque rich cream, #655 opaque green, #722 opaque orange, #721 opaque yellow, and #723 opaque red. Also shown are adorable matching turtle earrings done in brick stitch.

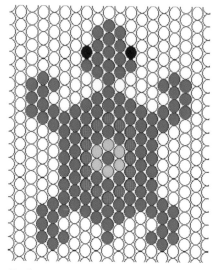

Turtle Pattern

Sheila Vinson's black pattern with the Ojo de Dios (God's eye) design uses Delica #10 opaque black, #653 pumpkin, #651 squash, #787 transparent matte blue, #200 opaque white, #723 opaque red, and #659 opaque blue.

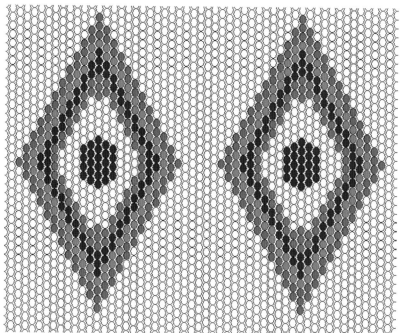

Ojo de Dios Pattern

This unique thunderbird pattern by Shelia Vinson was made with bold, bright colors. She used Delica #721 opaque yellow, #878 opaque turquoise, #722 opaque orange, #726 opaque cobalt blue, and #723 opaque red.

Alternate Thunderbird Pattern

12 Waterbird Tobacco or Medicine Bag

The waterbird frequently appears in ceremonial beadwork. Associated with peyote ceremonies of the Native American Church, the waterbird can be equated with the Holy Spirit concept in Christianity. The waterbird, facing upward, is seen as a messenger to the Creator, carrying the prayers of those participating in the ceremony. Often incorporated into beadwork designs, you'll see feathers signifying blessings, prayers, or spiritual protection.

Another popular Native symbol is the rainbow or use of rainbow colors to reflect light or the colors of daylight. Other images, like a cross, teepee, fire, cactus, arrowhead, mountains, and clouds, are prevalent in certain types of ceremonial beadwork. It is not unusual to see an American flag because many veterans are also honorable men and women held in high esteem within the Native community and church.

The waterbird is only one of many symbols sacred to Native American beaders. Native and non-Native beaders I know personally often tell me how they invest their hearts into their beadwork and why it holds much meaning for them. They describe how they willfully inject prayers and good thoughts intended to be passed on to the

eventual receiver of the beadwork. The beading process, considered to be both creative and spiritually inspired, is generally said to be highly rewarding in a very subjective sense. The process and the product both hold significance because of the power inherent in the symbolism.

This waterbird beadwork was designed to embellish a medicine bag. Although not all Native Americans recognize or use the same types of plant medicines, one very common sacred plant that has been used for more than a thousand years is tobacco. It is used in ceremonies to carry prayers to our Creator. Tobacco ties, tobacco offerings, and communal smoking from a ceremonial pipe are ways of using tobacco in a good way. Natives believe that there are no health risks when tobacco is used appropriately in the proper manner. Tobacco used in a nontraditional way, everyday, as promoted commercially, carries numerous health risks because of the addictive nature of nicotine. Ceremonial blends used for smoking often contain other healing herbs besides tobacco.

It's interesting to note that tobacco as a medicinal plant has been used for many conditions including such things as rheumatism, eczema, toothache, swollen throat, and even as a cure for colds, especially if the tobacco was mixed with desert sage. Remember that the Native American concept of medicine used here includes the treatment of physical as well as mental, emotional, and spiritual ills.

MATERIALS

- I tube each of Delica or hex beads in opaque rainbow colors (black, dark blue, light blue, green, yellow, orange, red, white) and a background color (we use #238 turquoise with AB finish)

- size 10 or 12 beading needle

- size A or O beading thread

- clear nail polish

- leather medicine bag

- leather or fabric glue

BASIC STITCHES

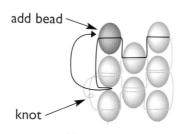

Odd-Count Flat Peyote Stitch

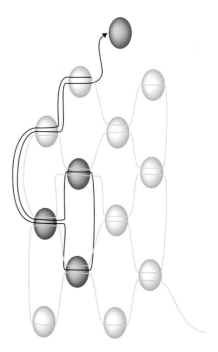

Triangle Turnaround

Project Notes

This beadwork is seen on a leather medicine bag, but it can be used in many ways. Traditional ceremonial uses include on a tobacco bag, a pipe bag, or an altar cloth. It is also seen adorning the fan, rattle, or other paraphernalia used in the ceremony itself.

Common medicinal herbs that might be stored in such a bag include sage, sweet grass, and copal. People who use modern medicines may carry a medicine bag with prescribed pharmaceuticals, such as nitroglycerin or blood-pressure-lowering medication for treating heart disease or equipment needed for insulin injection for treating diabetes.

Although instructions are not included on how to assemble the leather bag, if you want to make your own, find a bag pattern on page 118. Of course, you may prefer to buy a leather or fabric bag that's already assembled. The beadwork can also be used as a pendant for a fancy necklace with fringe or backed with leather and made into an armband or choker. You can add a little leather fringe to your bag if you wish.

This project will teach you how to do odd-count flat peyote stitch and decreasing flat peyote stitch. Generally speaking, even-count peyote-stitch patterns are preferable because they are simpler to make. However, a pattern will occasionally require an uneven number of beads so that the project has the proper symmetry.

If you have experience with even-count flat peyote, you'll know what the beads look like at the end of the first two rows. With odd-count, the stitch is essentially the same except that when you reach the end, there is no apparent place to attach the last bead. The method shown will help you see a way to attach the last bead to finish the row.

Triangle turnaround is a technique used for decreasing with odd-count flat peyote stitch.

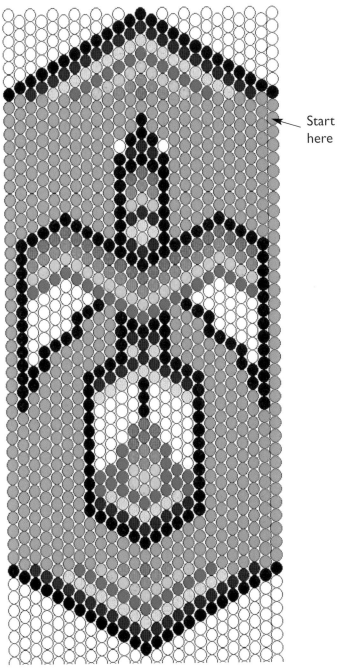

Start here

Waterbird Pattern

1. Starting where the arrow is marked on the pattern, put 25 beads on your needle, with the thirteenth (middle) bead black. We will call this the first row. You'll be working the pattern from the top down. Similar to even-count flat peyote, you will be adding one bead every other bead. Pick up one bead, skip the first bead, and pass your needle through the next bead.

2. When you get to the end of the second row, you'll find that there are two loose beads, with no place to attach the beads that you are adding. At this point, tie a square knot with your two pieces of thread. Secure it with clear nail polish and do not trim the end until the nail polish is dry.

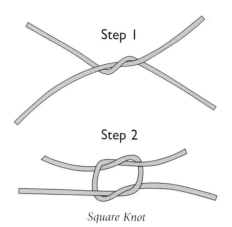

Square Knot

3. After the nail polish is dry, change directions of your thread by running your needle through the last bead added.

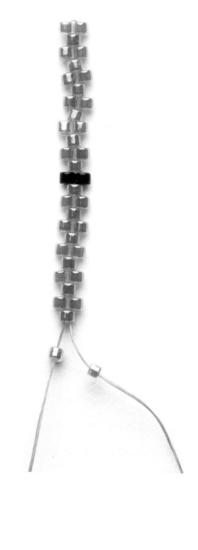

4. Continue beading to finish the third row, following the pattern to know the order of bead colors to pick up.

5. When you get to the end of the fourth row, you will again face the dilemma of having no place to attach the last bead. Place your needle under the thread bridge on the side of rows 1 and 2 and then change directions by passing your needle through the last bead added. This procedure will be required every other row. Be careful with your thread tension so that your beadwork does not curl and buckle. Take a deep breath so that you relax your own tension. You want beadwork that is even and flat.

See the triangle turnaround drawing on page 76.

6. When you have completed the main design, you will need to finish the tapered points by decreasing with flat peyote stitch. This necessitates a one-bead decrease at the beginning and end of each row. To decrease, you will skip over the last bead by weaving your thread through 3 beads in a triangle and changing direction of your thread path so that your

needle exits the appropriate bead. Keep your thread tension snug so the thread doesn't show but not so tight that you buckle your beadwork.

7. After you have finished both sides, you're ready to mount the beadwork onto your leather. It is preferable that the beadwork is attached before the leather bag is sewn together, because the beadwork will be attached temporarily with a very thin layer of leather or fabric glue and tacked down to the leather with discreet stitches. Colored thread that blends well with the bag will help prevent the thread from showing. An alternative glue is a supple jewelry or fabric adhesive that is pliable when dry, not stiff like epoxy types of cements.

Caution: Stiff glue will ruin your beadwork and your leather bag!

13

Huichol-Lace
Sun Catcher

*H*uichol beaders are recognized worldwide for their exquisite beadwork. Renowned for gourd beadwork, they also produce bracelets, earrings, barrettes, and medicine bags with both flat and circular netting.

Gourd beadwork originates from ceremonial experiences. Many designs originated from peyote visions and have been recorded to honor a type of spiritual communication. The technique involves pressing glass beads into a beeswax lining on the inside of a bowl-shaped gourd.

The colors and designs are significant since they represent traditional symbols and ceremonial visions. Their ancestral spirits are honored by using symbolic manifestations of nature in their artwork, such as the deer, corn, eagles, serpents, earth, sun, fire, water, and peyote. Unfortunately, traditional sacred objects are sometimes transformed into commercial art, which can be a source of conflict for many traditionalists.

The Native American gourd bowls are highly prized because of their intricate detail and bright, colorful designs. The gourd itself, fashioned into a prayer bowl, symbolizes the womb of mother earth, capable of swelling with the creation of new life. The Huichol also produce beaded masks and beaded ironwood carvings of mostly animal figures.

Since the style of pressed beadwork is extremely difficult to imitate, I mention it only to provide insight into the Huichol art form and its ritual uses. The netting technique featured in this project is also an art form with similar attraction for the tourist market. However, it is clear that items like hair clips, bracelets, and earrings are typically small items with limited space for elaborate designs other than geometric patterns. A rare find is a beaded medicine bag that's likely to bear significant symbolism.

MATERIALS

- size 11 seed beads, assorted colors (silver-lined and transparent colors recommended)
- size 3 bugle beads, at least one color
- size B or A thread
- size 10 beading needle
- scissors
- clear nail polish

BASIC STITCH

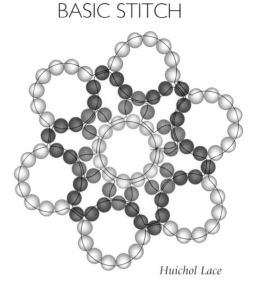

Huichol Lace

Project Notes The sun-catcher ornament is versatile as a jewelry component. With a little creativity, you can use the same kind of beadwork for earrings with elaborate fringe, window dressings like curtain tiebacks, Christmas ornaments, pins, and hair decorations, like ties for braids. The sun-catcher ornament can also be used as a bracelet or necklace pendant. Larger beads, like size 6 pony beads, and heavier cord, like artificial sinew, can be used to make larger ornaments for children. Although nail polish is recommended as a stiffening agent for seed beads, heavier and larger beads will require a fabric stiffener or another product that dries clear.

After you learn how to discriminate between rows, you can use more than one color of bead per row and create many interesting patterns. Don't be afraid to experiment to make your own unique creations.

The pattern here may be seen as a flower, star, or sun symbol. The bright colors of the beads reflect light and make an attractive window decoration. The different stages of construction show different earring designs, some emphasizing circular floral shapes or lace and some emphasizing star shapes or sun shapes with spokes or rays of light. Try reflecting the light of your own personality by using a rainbow of colors to create your own designs. The project design uses different colors throughout so that you can clearly see which row you are adding.

Huichol lace is also called open-lace netting.

1. Thread about 1 yard of thread on your needle. Pick up 12 beads of one color and tie them in a ring with a square knot. Secure the knot with clear nail polish and let it dry.

2. Pick up 3 beads of a different color, skip a bead, and pass your needle through the next bead. Continue adding 3 beads every other bead until you finish the ring.

3. At the end of each row, pass your needle to the peak (top) bead from the previous row. Add 5 beads from peak to peak. Tie an in-line (half-hitch) knot at the end of every row to keep your thread tension taut.

4. Pick up 7 beads (using 2 light beads, 3 dark, and 2 light for the 7 beads) and pass your needle from peak to peak.

5. This row is different. Pass your needle through the first 2 beads of the previous row, add 5 beads, and pass your needle into the sixth bead (or second from the end of a 7-bead group). Continue adding 5 beads from the sixth bead to the second bead of the next 7-bead group and the second bead to the sixth bead for a total number of 12 peaks. Your beadwork will begin to look wavy, but it will look better with continuing rows.

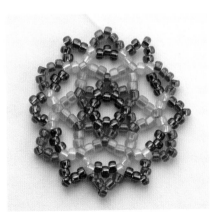

6. For the next row, add 5 beads from peak to peak.

7. For the next row, add 5 beads from peak to peak.

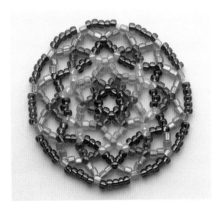

The table on the next page shows an abbreviated version of the number of beads per row.

Row 1	12 beads in a ring
Row 2	Add 3 beads every other bead for a total of 6 peaks
Row 3	Add 5 beads from peak to peak.
Row 4	Add 7 beads from peak to peak.
Row 5	Add 5 beads from the second to the sixth and the sixth to the second to the end of the row of 12 peaks.
Row 6	Add 5 beads from peak to peak
Row 7	Add 5 beads from peak to peak

VARIATIONS

The design shown here is not the only Huichol lace design you could make. Some designs begin with a ring of 8 to 10 beads, which creates a tighter appearance with fewer open spaces. The bracelet in Chapter 14 has a beaded ornament that uses bugle beads to create a more defined star shape. Try experimenting with the placement of different colored beads to create many unusual designs.

Angelique Alvarez made the brown and gold necklace pedant.

8. To finish your sun-catcher ornament, spray or dip it in distilled water, shape it, and let it dry. After it dries thoroughly, use clear nail polish to stiffen the threads. Use more than one coat if necessary and allow the ornament to dry thoroughly between coats. Tie it with a pretty ribbon or metallic thread and hang it in a nearby window. Try using size 6 pony beads and artificial sinew to make large ornaments.

The two gourd bowls were recently acquired from a Huichol Indian art trader. In order to achieve even greater detail in their artwork, the traders provided the artists size 14 beads, which are very small.

14

Ladder-Chain Bracelet

LADDER STITCH

BEGINNER

*T*he simple ladder stitch provides a basic foundation for many types of beaded earrings and bracelets. Although it does not hold any profound meaning or symbolism, it's often one of the first beadwork stitches ever learned. The ladder stitch is very functional, as you'll see with project samples. The ladder-chain bracelet project will show you how to use the stitch to make a variety of objects with different sizes and types of beads. Bugle beads are usually used to form the base of triangular earrings. When the same stitch is used with seed beads, it looks entirely different.

This project shows you how to make a simple bracelet with an embellished edge. You'll also learn how to combine the ladder stitch with circular netting from Chapter 13 to make an interesting bracelet or pendant. The chain can also create three-dimensional objects, like an ornament cover or a strap for a bag or pendant. We invite you to explore combining different techniques to expand your beadwork creations.

A common Native American earring design has a triangle top with fringe and uses the ladder stitch at the base with bugle beads instead of seed beads. Due to their popularity with tourists, they have been widely distributed in the retail market. These Apache-weave earrings are often simply called American Indian earrings. The weave and design is often the first project beginning Native and non-Native beaders attempt.

MATERIALS

- bugle beads, size 3

- seed beads or faceted beads, such as size 8, 10, or 11, for edging (use a variety of types)

- clasp

- size B or O thread

- beeswax (to help with thread tension)

- size 10 or 12 beading needle

- clear nail polish

- scissors

Project Notes

This simple bracelet is great for beginners because they experience a sense of accomplishment by making an attractive piece of jewelry. More experienced beaders can introduce variations shown on page 88.

Step 1

Step 2

Step 3 Reinforcing the base

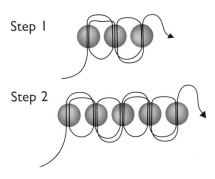

Ladder Stitch

1. Place about 1 yard of thread on your needle and pick up 1 bugle bead, 1 seed bead, 1 bugle bead, 1 seed bead, 1 bugle bead, 1 seed bead, and an end of the clasp.

Tie your beads into a triangle and tie a square knot to secure it. Glue the knot with clear nail polish.

2. With your needle coming out of one of the bugle beads, pick up another bugle bead and run your needle through the opposite end of the first bead.

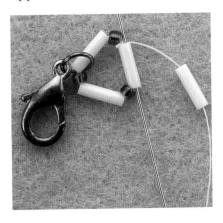

3. Move your needle by running it through the bead you just added.

4. Continue adding beads in this manner until you finish the length of the bracelet. An average woman's bracelet measures 7½ to 8 inches. Attach the other end of the clasp to the last bugle bead the same way you started (by adding one seed bead, one bugle bead, one seed bead, one bugle bead, and one seed bead.)

5. Finish the edging by adding 3 seed beads on the edge of every other bugle bead until you finish the length of the bracelet. You'll notice size 11 seed beads on the edge in the photo below. If you use larger beads, you can achieve a different look to your bracelet. Experiment by using a combination of bead sizes to see what fits and looks good to you.

VARIATIONS

This bracelet shows how you can combine the ladder stitch with the Huichol-lace sun-catcher ornament from Chapter 13 to make an interesting bracelet with a centerpiece.

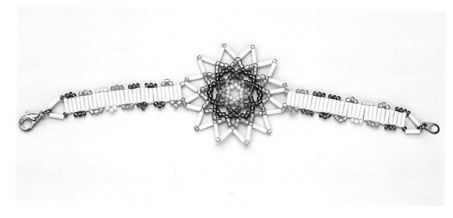

The ladder stitch with bugle beads is combined with Apache weave (brick stitch or stacking stitch) to make sleek and slinky earrings for evening wear.

Cherri Miller incorporated the ladder stitch into a three-dimensional ornament cover.

The pipe earrings, designed by Eric Johnson and beaded by Louise Johnson and Heather Bacon, are an example of beadwork that often begins with a row of ladder stitch.

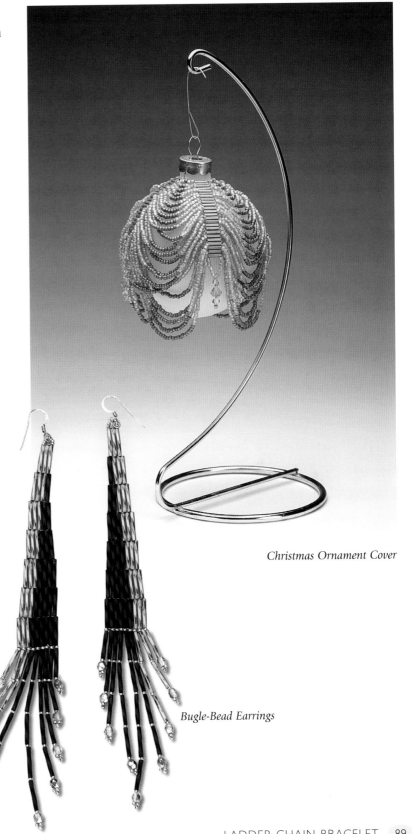

Christmas Ornament Cover

Pipe and Tomahawk Earrings

Bugle-Bead Earrings

15 Dream-Catcher Ornament

FRETTING AND DREAM-CATCHER WEBBING

INTERMEDIATE

The origin of the dream catcher or web is unclear, but many Native tribes use it, and other peoples throughout the world recognize it as a piece of art. Internet research suggests that the Ojibwe or Chippewa may have been the originators of the dream web. However, the dream catcher has clearly been adopted by many tribes across the continent as evidenced by its popularity in the Southwest. As the story is sometimes told, the web draws in and entangles negative energy, like bad dreams, so that the dreamer sleeps protected. Some type of crystal or glass, or a clear object, is woven into the center to allow the positive and good dreams to enter. The first rays of sunlight at dawn cause the bad dreams to evaporate. Other versions have a hole in the center which allows any nightmares to escape.

A dream state is somewhat difficult to define, other than as a given state of mental consciousness. Scientists can describe physiological changes, for rapid-eye-movement sleep, that can be measured to indicate that the sleeper is in a dream state. However, most people acknowledge their understanding of the dreamworld on an experiential basis.

Many parents actually use dream catchers in their homes and attest to their effectiveness. They are wildly popular with tourists. They are used for children as well as adults, especially for people who are vulnerable due to physical or emotional sickness. Perhaps it is useful as a spiritual tool to help individuals become aware of their place in the natural world in a quest for spiritual understanding. Even small children try to understand and cope with their fears of the unknown.

The ring or hoop that's the basis for the dream catcher represents the circle of life. The sacred hoop defines the cycles evident in nature from birth through death. It is also a symbol of the balance of nature and our relationship with the earth, the four-legged animals, sea life, winged creatures, and all of creation.

Traditionally, the hoop is made out of a willow, and the web is made of sinew or nettle-stalk cord, dyed red with bloodroot. Dream catchers are typically hung on the cradleboard of infants and eventually over the beds of youngsters. A piece of crystal may sometimes be used along with turquoise, bone beads, and feathers. The hoop may be wrapped with leather lace.

Many forms of dream catchers are nontraditional. Some employ fancy gemstones, neon-colored feathers, dyed artificial sinew, silver wire, and sterling charms.

MATERIALS

- 1-inch-diameter metal hoop with loop for hanging

- metallic thread or artificial sinew (available in craft, fiber or yarn, or sewing shops)

- size 10 to 12 beading needle

- size A or O beading thread

- size 11 beads, three or four colors

- size 14 beads, one color

- tube of 5-mm twisted bugle beads

- ten size 4-mm fire-polish beads

- clear nail polish

- split ring for hanging

- leather lace or Ultrasuede, 8 inches long

BASIC STITCH

Step 1
Pick up 3 beads.

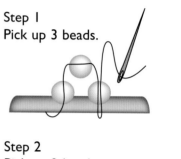

Step 2
Pick up 2 beads.

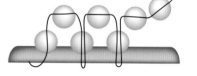

Fretting

Project Notes This project piece uses a multicolored metallic fiber, glass beads, and a metal hoop. The small beads used in the webbing look like stars floating in the universe. This pendant can be hung in any window to catch the light. You can also use it as a jewelry component.

Dream catchers are traditionally made out of natural materials like willow, leather, feathers, bone, animal sinew or plant fibers, and crystals or other gemstones. They were not typically used as jewelry, but the creative artist loves to experiment with different types of media and art forms. The dream catcher is popular in sterling wire earrings as well as a multitude of fiber and fabric arts, including clothing, quilts, and yarn woven into wall hangings. The dream catcher is also seen in gourd art (painted, etched, or woven), paintings, and pottery.

The metallic thread shown in this project is a multifilament thread that's somewhat delicate compared with sinew or heavier cords. Be brave and try experimenting with different types of fibers that can be mixed with beads to produce unusual dream catchers. Exotic materials can be found in fabric stores and yarn stores as well as craft supply stores. Consult with your favorite artists to see where they obtain their materials. Many types of unusual components like feathers, charms, and ornaments (bought or handmade) can be used as embellishments.

The beading technique is fretting or a fretting-edge stitch.

1. Measure about 2 yards of metallic thread and tie a square knot onto the top of the hoop. Secure the knot with clear nail polish.

2. Thread your needle and drape your thread across the front of the hoop. Pass your needle over the metal hoop, passing your needle under the left side of the thread. Use the markers on the hoop to space your thread evenly. Keep your tension tight by pulling your thread toward the center of the hoop.

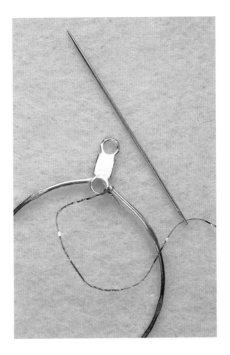

3. Continue all the way around the hoop until you reach the top of the hoop. Start your second row by passing your needle under the first thread loop and centering your thread before continuing.

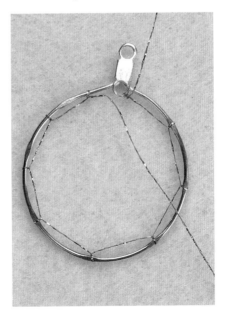

4. Starting with row 2, add a bead before looping your thread.

5. Continue with your webbing, pushing each bead from the previous row aside to the left before looping your thread around the previous loop.

6. When you have reached the center of the hoop, tie off your thread by adding an inconspicuous in-line (half-hitch) knot. Do not cut your thread. Secure the knot with clear nail polish.

7. Add the center dangle by placing 6 seed beads, one 4-mm bead, and three size 14 beads. Pass over the last 3 beads and go back up the other beads. Add 3 more beads to turnaround and add a second dangle. This center embellishment is optional. You can also add a silver feather, a turquoise chip, a bone feather, or any attractive assortment of beads.

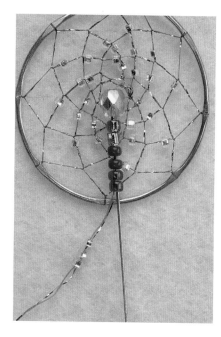

8. Thread your needle with beading thread. Although metallic thread is also acceptable, it's easier to use beading thread on the edging to minimize tangling and fraying. Tie a square knot at the top of the hoop (right thread over left thread and through the hole, then left thread over right thread and through the hole). Secure the knot with clear nail polish.

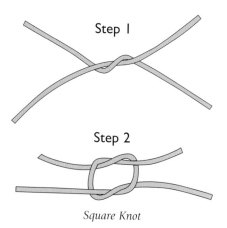

Step 1

Step 2

Square Knot

9. Pick up 7 seed beads on your needle. To secure the beads to the hoop, pass the needle under the hoop and back through the last 3 beads added (the seventh, sixth, and fifth beads). Tighten your thread by pulling up with your needle.

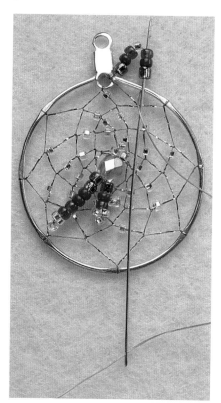

10. Pick up 4 more beads. Pass your needle under the hoop and back up through the last 3 beads added. You will see that the middle bead pops up as you continue adding beads in this manner all the way around the hoop.

11. When you have finished, tie an in-line (half-hitch) knot and secure with clear nail polish.
  Trim your thread when it is dry.

12. Add your fringe by finding the middle point and adding an even number of dangles on each side of the middle point.
  The photo, top left on page 95, shows the dangle consisting of 5 beads of each color, one bugle bead, one size 14 bead, one 4-mm fire-polish bead, and three size 14 beads.
  Do the turnaround by skipping over the last 3 beads added and passing your needle back through all the other beads strung.

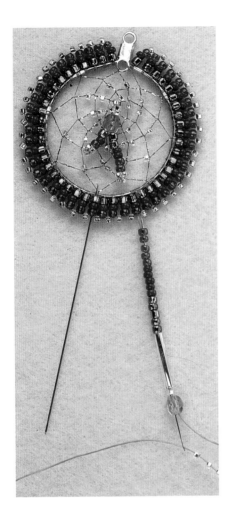

13. Move your needle to pass through the next set of edge beads and add another dangle until you have finished.

14. After finishing your fringe, add a split ring and leather lace or ribbon for hanging.

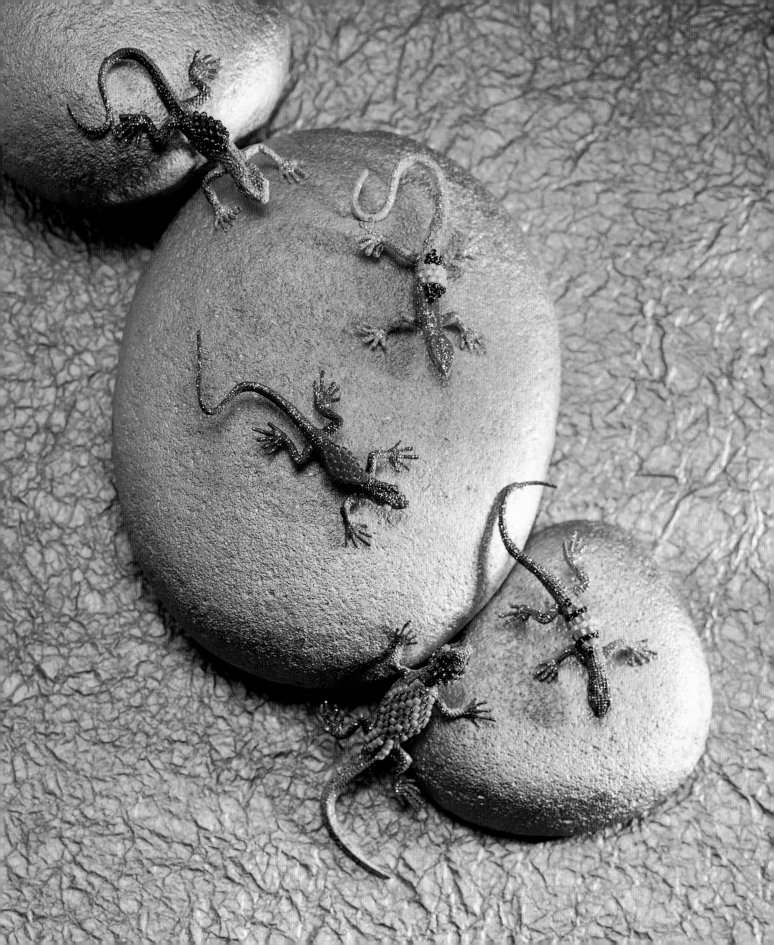

16

Southwest Gecko Pin

*T*his little creature, commonly called a gecko, has become an icon of Southwestern décor. The image is seen in fabric design, wall art, home decorations, and jewelry. The deserts of the Southwest, including the Mojave and Sonoran deserts of southeastern California, southwestern Arizona, and southern Nevada, are home to many lizards and other reptiles. They're also found in the rocky or sandy desert and semiarid regions in southwestern Utah, southwestern New Mexico, and northern Mexico.

Lizards are traditional symbols of longevity. These beautiful and delicate creatures often have fascinating colors and patterns on their skin that are sometimes translucent. Most geckos are nocturnal and avoid the heat of the day. They hide underground in rock crevices and rodent burrows, eating insects, spiders, baby scorpions, and other small arthropods lower on the food chain.

MATERIALS

- plastic gecko (lizards, frogs, or other amphibians from toy stores and novelty shops)
- size 11 seed beads, two colors for the body and one for the eyes
- bottle of glitter paint (available at craft stores)
- paintbrush
- pin back
- jewelry adhesive
- size 10 beading needle
- size A or O beading thread
- clear nail polish
- scissors

BASIC STITCHES

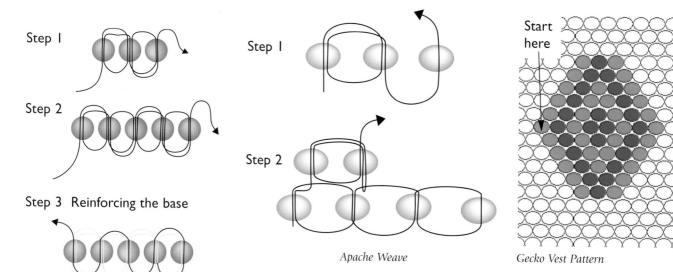

Step 1

Step 2

Step 3 Reinforcing the base

Ladder Stitch

Step 1

Step 2

Apache Weave

Start here

Gecko Vest Pattern

Project Notes This simple beginner project recognizes that the smallest creatures in nature have their beauty. The molded-plastic gecko usually ranges in size from about 2 to 6 inches long, including the tail. Here we bead and paint the gecko with hot colors to make a sparkling piece of jewelry to pin to your shoulder, handbag, or jacket. Or just let him crawl about on a bookshelf or coffee table or dine with him sitting near placemats. He can decorate houseplants or loll about your desk or computer to add a little whimsy to your work environment.

Shiny beads form a sort of vest or jacket for the gecko or lizard. We've added shimmering body paint to make this fellow from the Southwest into a colorful accent.

Apache weave is also called stacking stitch or brick stitch. This project also uses ladder stitch.

1. Begin by picking up 2 beads on your needle and pass the needle back through the first bead added, as shown in the photo at right. The width will vary, depending on the width of the plastic gecko's back. The project sample is about ½ inch wide, and the beadwork is 8 beads wide. If you need your base to be bigger, increase the number of beads to fit. Since this gecko jacket is diamond-shaped (two triangles, top and bottom) begin with the base row or the center row, the widest part of the diamond. We'll decorate our gecko with a beaded vest or jacket and then add paint and eyes. Read the pattern by starting at the widest point as shown by the arrow. This is your center or base row, the widest part of the diamond. (See Introduction for how to read a beading pattern.)

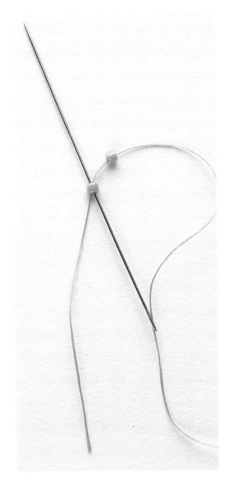

2. Move your needle down the second bead and pick up the third bead, following the pattern. Pass your needle through the third bead and add another bead the same way.

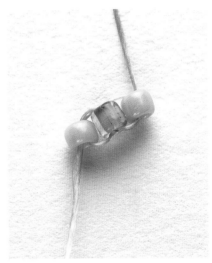

3. After finishing the base row of the beaded diamond, try it on the back of the gecko to make sure it is wide enough. Weave your needle back to the first bead to reinforce your base row.

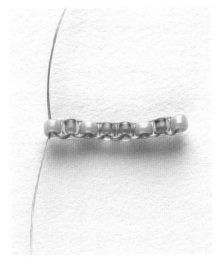

4. Finish the top of the triangle by using the Apache weave. In the beginning of the row, pick up 2 beads. Pass your needle under the second thread bridge and go up the second bead, down the first bead, and back up the second bead. I call this the "up-down-up thing." (See Apache weave step 2.)

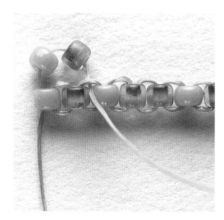

5. Continue adding beads one at a time by going under the thread bridge and back up the bead just added. The stitch automatically decreases by one every row. Keep adding rows until you complete the top row,

which has 3 beads. Weave your thread to the base row to complete the bottom half.

6. When you finish the rows, you'll have a diamond shape, which will be somewhat flat. The 3 strands of fringe for tail embellishment are optional.

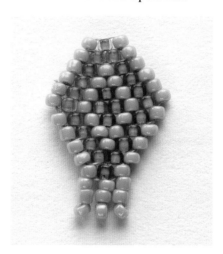

7. Run your needle and thread all around the edge of the beadwork, pulling slightly as you go to curve the edge of the diamond shape. When you have a nice shape, tie off with an in-line (half-hitch) knot and secure the knot with clear nail polish.

In-line Knot

8. With jewelry adhesive, attach the beadwork to the back of your gecko. You'll notice that the beadwork is somewhat flexible, so you can easily shape it to fit around the back of the plastic gecko.

9. After the glue dries, you're ready to add glitter paint. This special paint dries clear but leaves the colored glitter to shimmer and accent the underlying color. Glitter paint can also be used as an adhesive for beads attached as eyes. Use tweezers or a toothpick to attach the eyes to the paint. The paint can be used to add a new color to your gecko or to accentuate an existing color.

10. As a final step, use jewelry adhesive to attach a pin back to the belly of your gecko, that is, if you plan on using the little fellow as a pin.

VARIATIONS

A female gecko can also be adorned with nail polish on her toes, and she can wear her own jewelry, such as a beaded necklace and bracelet. But we know you won't need any more hints.

17 Sage Bear Sachet

WHIP STITCH AND APPLIQUÉ

BEGINNER

According to Native legends, the bear has been a powerful ally noted for teaching humans the many medicinal uses of plants that allow us to maintain good health in balance with nature. Sage is an important plant bears have introduced. To honor the great bear, we're shaping this sage sachet just like him.

Throughout the world, sage has been used to treat various meats in order to prevent bacterial infection. We're most familiar with this herb flavoring traditional Thanksgiving turkey feasts. Sage comes in dozens of varieties, several of which are particularly good for culinary uses. Common names include desert sage, purple sage, garden sage, white sage, and tricolor sage.

The different sage varieties boast an array of fragrances, including musky, sweet lavender, and rose-flavored essences. The plant's essential oil helps treat ailments such as skin lesions or lice. Medical practitioners have noted that the plant improves blood flow and has been used to treat conditions like high blood pressure and impotence. The dried plant can be brewed into a tea or consumed as a powdered leaf.

Sage has been used to treat indigestion, mental exhaustion, anxiety, and memory impairment. As a mouthwash, it treats sore throats and gum disease. Noted for its antimicrobial and antiviral effects, during the Middle Ages, sage was one of the herbs used to prevent the spread of the plague.

Natives and non-Natives have burned sage leaves and prayed to cleanse negative thoughts and influences. Synonyms for the word sage *are the words* wise *and* knowledgeable. *The smell of sage is said to attractive positive people and thoughts while disturbing or agitating negative or evil forces. As one Navajo child described the smell of the sacred herb, "It smells like angels dancing in my head."*

BASIC STITCHES

MATERIALS

- 12 x 12-inch square piece of leather or Ultrasuede
- size 11 or 8 seed beads
- size 2, 3, or 5 bugle beads in any color
- size 10 beading needle
- size A, O, or B thread
- sage or other aromatic herbs or flowers for stuffing the sachet

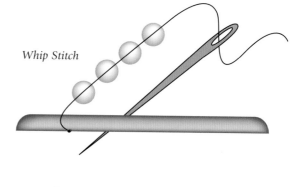

Whip Stitch

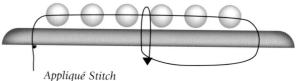

Appliqué Stitch

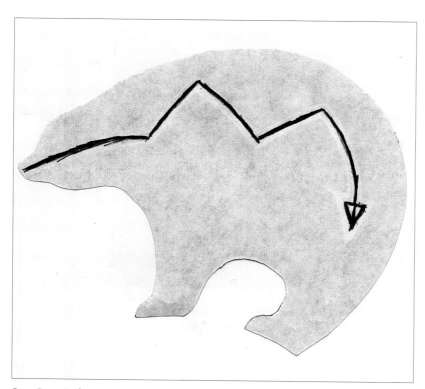

Sage Bear Sachet Pattern

Project Notes This project combines the powerful bear symbol and the use of the herb sage to make an embellished pillow or sachet.

Aromatic scents are used to calm the spirit and relax the body. This type of sachet is often used in dresser drawers and closets to add a good fragrance to clothing and to the room. It is also used at bedtime to tuck under a bed pillow to aid in restful sleep. Pick your favorite colors and make something special for yourself or someone you love.

This project uses whip stitch and appliqué. Whip stitch is sometimes called wrap stitch, and appliqué stitch is also sometimes referred to as couching.

1. Trace two images of the bear pattern onto your leather or fabric with a marker, pen, or pencil and cut them out with sharp scissors. We will be beading onto the front of one piece only and then sewing the two pieces together with a beaded edge.

2. Thread your needle with a comfortable length of thread, about one yard. Tie a knot in your thread and bring your needle through the fabric from back to front, so that your knot won't show. Following the inside pattern line, string one size 8 seed bead, one bugle bead, and one seed bead. Tack these beads down by running your needle through the fabric from front to back. For a neater appearance, tack down each bead by passing your needle over the thread between each bead.

3. Using the pattern as a guide, finish sewing the beads in place. We've made a row of alternating seed and bugle beads with a row of seed beads just below it. If you want more texture, try out different sizes and shapes of beads. Don't be nervous about being creative or seeing what looks good.

Be careful to discard beads that are broken or chipped since they will cut the thread. Don't sew too tightly; if you do, your beadwork could pucker the fabric.

whole piece

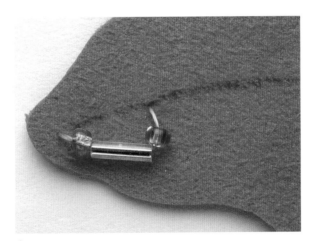

close-up

4. After you're finished with the surface beading, you can apply beads to the edge. Tie a knot in your thread and run your needle from the back to front of one piece only. Holding both pieces together, pick up three size 8 beads or four size 11 beads and run your needle from back to front through both pieces of fabric. Continue beading all the way around the edge until only about a 2-inch opening remains.

Stuff your pillow, through the opening, with fragrant herbs or dried flowers. Finish beading the edge.

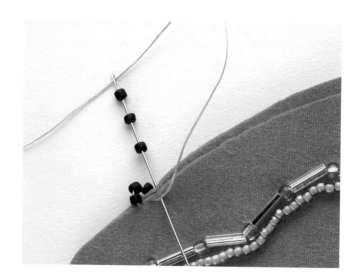

Native American Maiden

When the early Europeans arrived on this continent, like tourists arriving in Native lands in later centuries, they were fascinated by the unusual culture and beautiful pieces of artwork created by Native artists. Since then, collectors of all cultural backgrounds have supported Native art and artists from the 16th century to the present. The events of history have had a profound impact on the culture and art of Native peoples.

Through the centuries many Native artists have produced trinkets expressly for the tourist market. These trinkets have no real function, ceremonial or otherwise, in Native culture. In lean times as well as fat, these popular fancies have been traded for essential commodities like food or clothing. Native artwork, like that generated by other cultures, can indeed be influenced by what sells.

The adorable Native American maiden designed for this project has been styled after the traditional Apache camp dress that's often decorated with sewing trim called rickrack. The child proudly wears moccasins, braids, a silver necklace, and turquoise jewelry. This beaded image represents the innocence of youth and the optimism for new generations.

The image of a child, even more than that of a beautiful woman or man, is likely to instill empathy, sympathy, or love. Neutral objects like baskets or earrings do not typically ignite hostile emotions. As reflected in the commercial doll industry world-wide as well as in our hearts, children are recognized as symbols of innocence and vulnerability. Dolls, like little creatures—turtles, frogs, and even bugs—appear cute and seemingly harmless.

If dolls or images of animals once held symbolic meaning for a given culture, that fact may be irrelevant to the retail market today. From a cultural perspective, Kachina dolls are still used to teach powerful social or spiritual lessons to children.

Frogs and other water creatures are used symbolically in healing ceremonies. Turtles are used to represent longevity. A newborn baby's umbilical cord is sewn into the leather or fabric fetish and hung on cribs and cradleboards.

A child from any culture is precious and lovable. For me, this Indian maiden or little girl represents all Native children who deserve to be loved and nourished physically, intellectually, and spiritually. For any culture to survive, children must be held in highest esteem and protected with all the resources of the culture. And so, the symbolism of this little doll is indeed priceless.

MATERIALS

- tube of Delicas, hair color (black or brown)
- Delica beads, two colors for dress (turquoise and red)
- 6 silver beads for necklace
- rose bead for mouth
- tube of Delica beads, skin color
- tube Delicas, moccasin color
- size 10 or 12 beading needle
- size A or O beading thread
- metal pin back
- jewelry adhesive
- fringe beads (optional)

BASIC STITCHES

Step I

Step 2

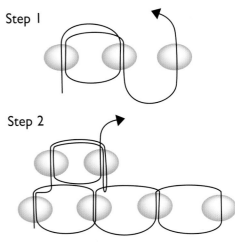

Apache Weave

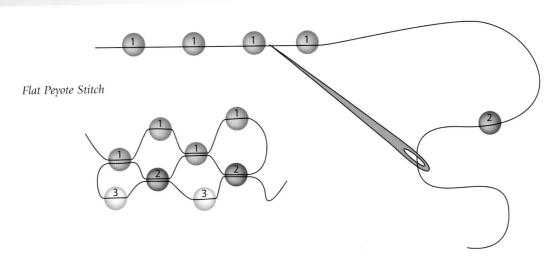

Flat Peyote Stitch

Project Notes This project requires increasing and decreasing at various points in the pattern. Apache weave or brick stitch has the characteristic of automatically decreasing every row, so you have to be concerned mainly when you need to increase. In general, it's best to choose a starting point for an Apache-weave design at the widest part of the pattern. (See the Introduction for how to read a bead pattern.) The starting point for this pattern was chosen to show you how to decrease and then increase. The first step shows a method for forming a stable base, which is actually rows 1 and 2. You will be working your beadwork up toward the head, weaving your needle back down to the base, turning your work upside down, and finishing the skirt and feet.

This project can be made into a pin or earrings.

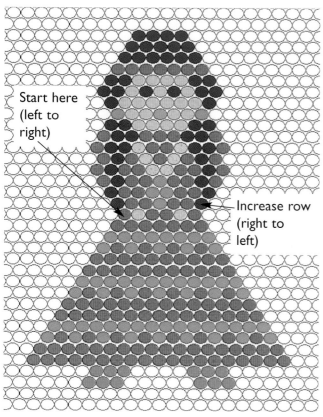

Indian Maiden Pattern 1

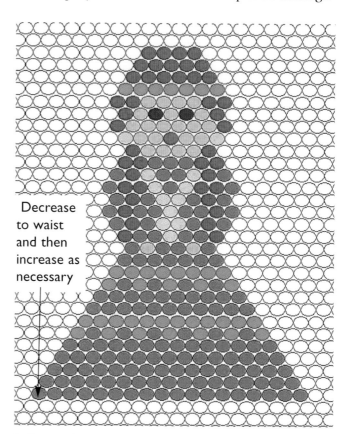

Indian Maiden Pattern 2

1. Starting at the arrow marked on the pattern, pick up 3 beads and pass your needle back through the first bead strung. Your beads will form a neat little triangle. Tie your thread into a square knot to stabilize your bead embryo. Seal the knot with clear nail polish. Do not trim the thread tail until thoroughly dry.

2. To form the base of the skirt, we will be adding one bead at a time to form a 2-bead row of flat peyote stitch. Continue adding beads according to the pattern until you finish the base.

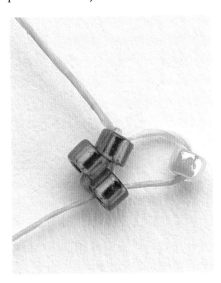

3. The third row requires increasing, which is done by adding 2 beads and going under the first thread bridge.

4. Then pass your needle up the second bead, down the first bead, and up the second bead. (This describes the thread path for beginning each row of Apache weave.) This action prevents the thread from showing on the side edges and helps to lock the beads in place so that they sit flat. With students, I've called this action the "up-down-up thing." It follows step 2 of the Apache weave.

5. Finish the row by adding only one bead at a time. Following the pattern, finish beading up to the top of the head.

6. Make the feather by having your needle exit the end bead on either side. Pick up 9 beads (3 white, 3 black, and 3 white) and run your needle down the second bead from the edge of the head. To shape your feather, do a square stitch on the first 3 beads on each side.

Square Stitch

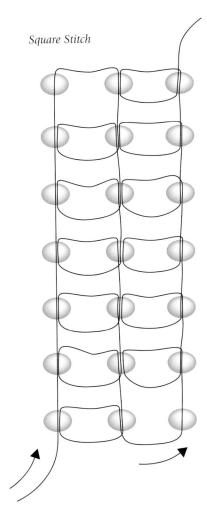

7. Weave your needle to the base row, turn the beadwork upside down, and continue following the pattern to finish the skirt. To make the moccasins, weave your needle through the beads to the appropriate spot on the pattern so that your thread does not show. Apache-weave one shoe and then the other, increasing or decreasing as necessary.

When you're all finished, you may stiffen your project with a thin coat of clear nail polish, if necessary. When the beads dry, use jewelry adhesive to glue on the metal pin back. The maiden with the purple outfit is an example of a fringed dress in lieu of moccasins.

VARIATIONS

Variations on this theme have included a few other American Indian images beaded by Native beaders. Lula Monroe beaded the men with headdresses (chiefs) and the fancy dancers (competition dancers). Genny Hatathlie beaded the Navajo woman in traditional red and blue dress. Indian dolls, angels, and even boys have been popular among tourists. Finally, the modern-looking Native woman with short hair and a green dress (with a fringe skirt) wears a concho belt and turquoise jewelry. The beader is unknown but probably Navajo, according to the trader from whom it was purchased.

Chiefs

Competition Dancers

Modern

Traditional

19 Blue Kokopelli Amulet Bag

ROUND PEYOTE STITCH

ADVANCED

*K*okopelli is back! This delightful character is loved around the world and characterizes the whole flavor of Southwest art. Also known as the flute player, Kokopelli has been found in petroglyphs from ancient times. He is also seen on antique ceramic pottery or shards (ceramic pieces) and kiva murals. Some Kokopelli flute-player images have humps on their backs, and some are without humps.

The flute-player image is recognized or interpreted as being a trader, warrior, insect, priest, gambler, holy man, or philanderer. Most typically, he is recognized as being a male and said to have power to bring rain. He is primarily known as a fertility symbol. The original pattern in this project is merely an interpretation of an ancient symbol.

A special use for this type of amulet or medicine bag is for a woman trying to get pregnant or trying to secure a mate. Medicinal herbs may be stored in it to help provide balance to the human body and may assist in securing a productive pregnancy.

Although the Kokopelli image has no magical powers, a woman can express her optimism through her personal prayers and request a blessing of fertility.

MATERIALS

- cardboard roll from toilet paper

- Delica or cylinder beads, color #10 black, #685 pink rose, #694 lavender, and #985 blue

- size 10 or 12 beading needle

- size A or O beading thread

- embellishment beads for fringe and strap

- transparent tape

- scissors

BASIC STITCHES

Step 1

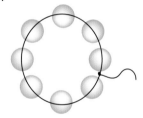

Step 2

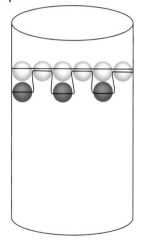

Round Peyote Stitch

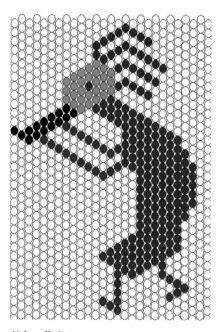

Kokopelli Pattern

Project Notes This pattern has 60 beads around and 35 beads from top to bottom. The finished bag is about 2½ inches long and 1½ inches wide. The image is beaded on the front of the bag, and the back is a solid background color. Some beaders enjoy duplicating the image on the back or making the bag reversible by putting another design on the back.

Since this is an advanced project, instructions for the fringe and strap are not included. Suggestions for the neck strap are a peyote rope (Chapter 6); circular netted rope (Chapter 10), or strung beads (Chapter 2).

As an alternative to a cardboard tube, you may be able to find a rounded plastic or glass medicine bottle that will accommodate 60 beads around it. If you need to make your bag a little larger to fit a medicine bottle, simply add an even number of beads to the background, making sure that your design is centered.

Round peyote stitch is also sometimes called circular peyote stitch.

1. Begin by stringing 60 background color beads on your needle and thread and tying a circle around the cardboard tube. Cut the tube lengthwise to get the perfect fit and tape it in place. Secure your knot with clear nail polish. Tape your thread tail in place to help you identify the beginning of your pattern. Move your needle over one bead by passing it through the first bead strung. Following the pattern, add one bead every other bead. In other words, pick up a bead on your needle, skip a bead, and pass your needle through the following bead. Continue all the way around the circle.

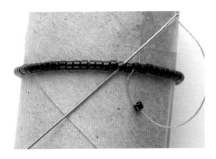

2. When you get to the end of the row, you will "drop down" to the next row by passing your needle through the first bead of the last row added. Continue following the pattern by adding one bead every other bead.

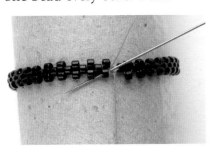

3. When you get to the bottom of the pattern, add 6 more rows, using flat peyote stitch. You will be making the bottom flap by beading only across 30 beads on either the front or the back of the bag. When you are finished with the flap, sew the bottom together by running your needle through the front and back of the bag in a zipper stitch. (For the zipper stitch, see the photo in Chapter 6, end of step 7.) To seam the beadwork, all you need to do is to run your needle and thread through the pop-up beads from side to side.

The photo at right shows how you can use an appropriate size of medicine bottle instead of a cardboard tube.

4. Finish your bag with fringe and a strap with many creative variations.

VARIATION

The pattern can also be beaded in flat peyote to make a pendant for a necklace or pin. Here's the same pattern created with different colors of beads (#37 silver lined copper, #985 teal, #685 rose, #694 purple, #862 blue). See page 10.

BAG PATTERNS

*White Buffalo Medicine Bag Pattern
(Chapter 3)*

*Waterbird Tobacco Bag or
Medicine Bag Pattern
(Chapter 12)*

BEADWORK GLOSSARY

abalone a type of shell that's polished, drilled, and used as a bead or button. It is highly prized by beaders and jewelry makers because its lustrous finish is similar to the natural coating found on pearls.

Apache weave a beading technique also called brick stitch, stacking stitch, Comanche weave, or Cheyenne weave. It is frequently used to make earrings with a triangular top since the stitch automatically decreases by one bead every row.

appliqué a sewing term that's used in beadwork to describe a method for sewing beads onto leather or fabric.

artificial sinew a stringing material made of waxed polypropylene.

aurora borealis a rainbow finish applied to beads.

badge clip a piece of hardware, sometimes called a finding, used to attach an identification badge to a necklace or neck strap.

bead finishes color or coating applied to the outside of beads. Many combinations or finishes, such as transparent frosted aurora borealis or silver-lined matte, are available. Glass beads may also have opaque, transparent, ceylon, frosted, iridescent, metallic, luster, luminous, or satin finishes.

bead loom a wooden, plastic, or metal structure designed specifically for bead weaving. Looms are sold commercially, but you can easily construct one at home. Bead looms are useful for making large pieces of beadwork such as belts, hatbands, or bead strips for embellishing fabric or leather.

bead sizes commonly manufactured seed bead sizes are 8, 10, 11, 12, 13, 14, and 15. The smaller the size, the larger the bead. Conversely, the larger the size, the smaller the bead.

bead thread a special thread designed for weaving and stringing beads, usually made of a sturdy synthetic like nylon or polyester rather than a biodegradable natural fiber like cotton. It comes in a variety of colors and sizes, including A, O, B, D, and F. The size of thread required for a particular project depends on the size of the bead hole and the weight of the project. Waxed bead thread is available to improve the tension of the stitch. You can also buy thread conditioners that minimize tangles and knots. Bead thread is sold in bobbins, spools, and on cards.

bead types the main bead manufacturers are in Japan, Italy, France, and the Czech Republic. Unique bead types are created by adding a variety of finishes, shapes, and facets. Examples include charlottes, bugles, three-cuts, Delicas, hex beads, and white hearts. Seed beads are made from glass rods or canes cut to make individual beads. They are then heated to make smooth oval shapes, although some are slightly squared.

bead wire a wire cable that is coated with nylon. It comes in a variety of diameters or gauges. The size of wire required for a particular project depends on the size of the bead hole and the weight of the project.

beaded bead a bead that is covered with other beads or a bead that is created with other beads.

beading needles these differ from sewing needles because the size of the eye tends to be smaller to accommodate both the bead and the thread. Beading needle sizes usually coincide with the size of the bead. For instance, a size 10 needle works well with a size 10 bead. However, many people do not know that beading needles can be versatile because the hole size is more important than the bead size. A size 10 needle is a good generic size that can work for size 10, 11, and 12 beads. If you work with size 12 or 13 beads, try a size 12 needle. There are many types, sizes, lengths, and manufacturers of needles. A few types of beading needles are long and short fine beading needles, twisted-wire needles, big-eye needles, and glover's needles.

beeswax a natural thread conditioner that helps to minimize thread tangling and helps to preserve the life of the thread.

big-eye needle a special beading needle that separates in the middle to form a needle with a large eye for easier threading.

bone hair pipe a tubular bead made of bone or shell, also called bone hairpipe. Once considered a type of battle armor familiar in museum displays, it is now commonly seen in chokers and dance regalia.

brick stitch a beading technique also called Apache weave, Comanche weave, and stacking stitch. Although the flat, two-dimensional form of the stitch is most common, it can also be done in a circular, three-dimensional form.

bugle beads tubular glass beads that are a popular shape in jewelry design. They are most commonly found in 1 mm, 2 mm, 3 mm, and 5 mm sizes and are available in a variety of colors and finishes.

cabochon a highly polished and cut gemstone that is flat on one side for use as a jewelry component. Cabochons are often used with a precious-metal bezel or a beaded bezel.

cedar seeds seeds from a cedar tree that are drilled for use as beads. They are also called ghost beads because of their reported use during the historic Ghost Dance, which was once forbidden. The essential oil from the cedar tree that gives off its characteristic smell has medicinal antibiotic properties. Often referred to as Grandfather Cedar, the leaf is used in cleansing ceremonies.

ceylon beads a pearlized finish on beads that tend to be in pastel colors.

charlotte cuts a size 13 to 14 Czech seed bead that is hand-faceted and available in limited supply. These are beautiful, sparkly beads.

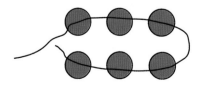

chile stitch a three-dimensional bead stitch also called log cabin, alligator, or gecko stitch. The specific origin of the stitch is uncertain, but many South American trinkets sold to tourists use this stitch. The chile (or chili) stitch refers to the chile pepper.

Chile Stitch step 1

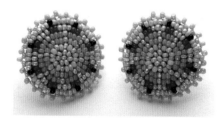

Chile Stitch step 2

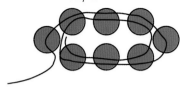

circular Comanche weave a beading stitch used for making round flat objects such as a necklace pendant.

circular netting a three-dimensional beading technique used to cover objects, like gourds. It can also form a three-dimensional shape, like a rope.

clasp hardware or finding used to close a necklace or bracelet.

Comanche weave a beading technique also called Apache weave, brick stitch, or stacking stitch.

concho a convex silver disk that sometimes has a button shank welded to it. Traditionally, sterling silver conchos were worn on a belt and used as money or a show of wealth.

cone a metallic finding used to cap strung beads in necklaces or earrings.

coral a semiprecious gemstone found in the ocean, usually seen in red, pink, white, or black. It is actually a petrified sea creature. Coral is regarded as a status symbol and is almost as popular as turquoise.

cotton cord a sturdy cord used for stringing beads and for straps. It is often dyed and waxed.

couching a method for sewing beads onto fabric.

cowry shells seashells often seen on beadwork as embellishment. They were once used like money or a medium of exchange imported or traded from other tribes.

crimper bead a special bead made of soft metal that collapses with pressure from flat-nosed pliers. It is used to secure a clasp or jewelry component when attached to bead-stringing wire.

crow beads large-holed glass beads often seen on leather fringe.

Delica a type of Japanese manufactured glass bead known for its laser-cut precision sizing and uniformity of shape. Delicas are also known as cylinder beads. Delica is the trademark of Miyuki Shoji Corp. The Toho Corp. manufacturers similar beads called Antiques, which, contrary to their name, are not old beads.

dentallium shell a dainty seashell that has a natural cavity for stringing.

donut a bead shape usually made from a gemstone to be used as a jewelry component.

dream-catcher hoop a ring made of metal that's sometimes wrapped with leather or beads. The hoop may also have a web woven from sinew or thread that's in turn decorated with beads and feathers.

dream-catcher webbing the inside of the dream-catcher hoop that is woven and often compared to a spider web.

drop down when working a round peyote-stitch pattern from the top down, you'll be required to pass a

Dream-Catcher Webbing

needle through the first bead added from the previous row in order to move down to begin the next row. This is also called a "step up" if you're working from the bottom up.

ear wire a jewelry finding or component for beaded earrings. Numerous styles, including posts, fish hooks, clip-ons, hoops, leverbacks, French wires, and custom designs, such as ear cuffs, are also considered ear wires.

edging stitch a method of applying beads to accent an edge of fabric, leather, or metal hoop.

eyeglass-holder findings adjustable plastic ends that secure your eyeglass arms.

eye pin a finding used to attach jewelry components.

eye screw a finding or hardware that is threaded for screwing into wood or gourds.

fetish an animal figure that is usually made of gemstone, silver, wood, clay, or shell. Some people attach significance to an animal trait(s) or

characteristic(s) to which they want to associate themselves or aspire to.

finding hardware used in jewelry construction such as eye pins, clasps, ear wires, jump rings, etc.

fire-polish beads faceted glass beads manufactured in the Czech Republic. They come in a large variety of colors and finishes. They are fired or heated to a very high temperature to smooth over the sharp facets, giving them a smooth but highly reflective surface.

flat headpin a metal pin with a flat base that is used in making earrings and jewelry.

flat netting an off-loom beading technique that is often seen in Huichol bracelets.

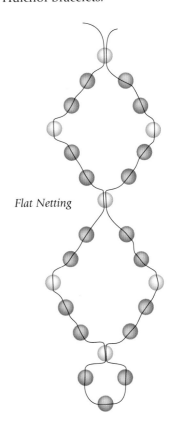
Flat Netting

flat-nose pliers a tool often used in jewelry making that has a smooth, flat jaw surface or a serrated, flat jaw surface. This tool is used for bending relatively soft wire or crimper beads.

flat-pad ear studs comfortable clutch-earring backs.

flat peyote stitch a two-dimensional beading technique that can be seamed to cover a three-dimensional object. It is often used for making bracelets and necklace straps.

flat round peyote stitch a beading technique used to make three-dimensional baskets.

free-form peyote stitch flat peyote stitch with different sizes of beads and accented with embellishment beads to make it more three-dimensional.

fretting a beading technique used to sew a beaded edge onto leather or fabric.

fringe strands of leather or beads used to hang from a beaded object or craft.

gecko a small reptile or lizard frequently called a water creature that is considered a symbol of longevity.

gem chips small pieces of gemstones that are polished and drilled for use as beads.

half-hitch knot also called an in-line knot because it places a knot in your thread exactly where you want to place it.

heishe (pronounced he-she) an old style of making beads from shell and gemstone chips, such as turquoise. The chips are individually drilled by hand and then strung on sinew, cord, or wire. They are then rolled to wear down the chips into a smooth strand of beads. It is a very arduous and lengthy process. Machines can create heishe beads, but the bead quality is usually inferior to those handmade.

hex beads abbreviation for hexagonal (six-sided) beads. The facets or cuts create a lot of subtle sparkle.

Peace pipe earrings with hex beads by Louise Johnson and Heather Bacon

hook clasp a common jewelry-closure finding; also called a hook and eye.

horizontal netting a beading technique done on the horizontal plane that is useful for covering oddly shaped three-dimensional objects.

Huichol a Native American tribe from Northern Mexico after which bead netting or Huichol lace is named.

Huichol lace a netting stitch, named after an American Indian tribe in Northern Mexico, which is also called horizontal, round, circular, or flat netting. It is also called open lace. Bead netting is similar to Huichol lace except for the shape. Huichol lace is round like a disk and bead netting is flat like a bracelet.

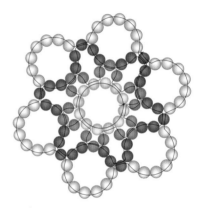

Huichol Lace

in-line knot a knot placed right in your thread to secure the beads and their tension. Also called a half-hitch knot.

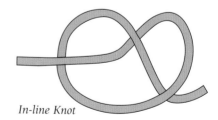

In-line Knot

inside-color beads transparent colored or clear beads with a different color inside.

iris beads beads with an iridescent finish.

jewelry cement a sturdy adhesive used for gluing glass, metal, and gemstones.

key ring a finding used for holding keys.

ladder stitch a beading stitch used to make a bead strip that resembles a ladder when made out of bugle beads.

leather lace long strips of thin leather used to make fringe, straps, and more.

lighter case a metal case used to hold a plastic lighter.

Lighter case

lobster-claw clasp a metal finding for attaching bracelets or necklaces.

loom stitch a stitch done on a bead loom. The finished work looks the same as square stitch, but loom stitch uses an entirely different technique.

luminous beads beads with neon or astro-brite colors inside the bead.

luster beads manufacturers' name for opaque beads with a pearllike finish.

matte-finish beads beads with a frosted, velvety, nonshiny texture on the outside.

metal earring hoop a metal hoop with a ring attached for adding an ear wire or charm.

metallic beads beads with a thin, shiny metal surface finish. Because the finish has a tendency to rub off, an acrylic fixative is recommended.

metallic thread a specialty thread made from metal filament that comes in a variety of colors.

memory wire a special wire made out of base metal that tends to hold its curved shape. It is a coarse wire that requires regular strong-cutting pliers (from the hardware store), not jewelry wire cutters. It is used to string rings, bracelets, and chokers. It is often referred to as wraparound jewelry since it is flexible and requires no clasp.

nail polish a clear acrylic liquid useful in beadwork for sealing knots on beading thread because of its delicate applicator brush.

needle-nose pliers a tool used for bending rings on soft wire to attach findings; also called round-nose pliers.

needles *See* beading needles.

netting a beading technique with subtle differences among the circular, horizontal, flat, round, and vertical styles and uses. *Circular netting* covers three-dimensional objects, like gourds, or forms a three-dimensional shape like a rope. *Horizontal netting* is woven on a horizontal plane, either flat like a necklace or three-dimensional like a Christmas ornament cover. *Flat netting* is usually two-dimensional like a bracelet.

Round netting is also flat like an ornament. (See Chapter 13) *Vertical netting* is woven on a vertical plane.

odd-count flat peyote stitch beadwork that has an odd number of beads in the pattern. (See Chapter 12.) The logistics for the stitch vary slightly from even-count peyote stitch.

off-loom weaving a number of stitches generally considered to be bead weaving that do not involve the use of a loom.

opaque beads solid-colored beads through which you cannot see light or thread.

peak bead refers to the center bead. For example, if you are adding five beads, the peak bead is the third or middle bead.

pearl knotting cord a special type of cord used for stringing and knotting between pearls. It is usually made of a synthetic, like polyester, but it is also made of silk and sold on a card with a needle attached.

petroglyph also called rock art, images are chiseled, etched, scratched, or pecked into boulders or rock formations.

peyote a cactus plant used in Native ceremonies.

peyote stitch a general term referring to several techniques for covering a three-dimensional object, also referred to as gourd stitch, round peyote, circular peyote, odd-count peyote, even-count peyote, flat peyote, round flat peyote, two-drop peyote, and three-drop peyote stitch.

pin back a piece of metal hardware that can be attached to the back of beaded jewelry.

pony beads glass beads often used for stringing projects.

pop-up beads in peyote stitch, when you add one bead every other bead, you'll notice that the new beads added will pop up or stick out more than those in the previous row. When you start the next row, it will be easy to identify the beads that you'll be adding new beads to because they are the "pop-up" beads.

porcupine quills hairlike structures used as beads.

right-angle weave a beadwork stitch that makes a chain with a foundation of four beads.

rosette a round beaded medallion that is a form of appliqué, used as a necklace pendant and as part of dance regalia.

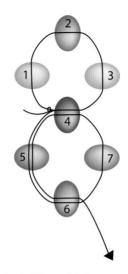

Right-Angle Weave Stitch

round-nose pliers a tool used for bending rings on soft wire to attach findings; also called needle-nose pliers.

round stitch a beading technique also called square stitch and corn stitch. This off-loom stitch is done in midair.

sculpted flat peyote stitch a technique for shaping beads into three-dimensional shapes.

Silamide waxed thread useful for stringing projects.

Rosette

silver-lined beads colored beads with a sparkly silver lining. These beads tend to have square holes that reflect light.

spacer bars bone, horn, hair, leather, or metal bars drilled with holes for stringing beads.

split ring a jewelry component used to attach a clasp to a bracelet or necklace.

square knot a common knot used for securing thread ends by tying your thread right over left and under the loop and then left over right and under the loop.

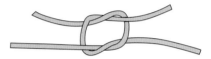

Square Knot

square stitch a beading technique also called corn stitch and round stitch. This is an off-loom stitch.

stacking stitch also called brick stitch, Apache weave, and Comanche weave.

step up when working a round peyote stitch pattern from the bottom up, you'll need to "step up," or pass your needle through the first bead added from the previous row. However, if you're working from the top down, this is called a "drop down."

stop bead a bead tied onto the end of beading thread to keep the other beads from falling off.

stringing wire nylon-coated wire cable used to string beads; available in a variety of gauges.

surgeon's knot a square knot with an extra loop at the top. This is a useful knot for elastic cord because it is a very tight knot that will not slip.

Surgeon's Knot

thread *See* bead thread.

thread bridge the small piece of thread between beads visible at the top of a row of beads, used to connect and anchor them. The Apache weave, or brick stitch, uses a thread bridge in the base row to anchor the beads for attaching the next row of beads.

tie tack a metal finding to pin a beaded object onto clothing like a tie, collar, or lapel.

transparent beads clear or colored beads that transmit light and allow you to see through them.

triangle beads three-sided glass beads.

"up-down-up thing" this describes the thread path for beginning each row of Apache weave or brick stitch. The technique prevents the thread from showing on the side edges and helps lock the beads in place so that they sit flat and straight.

vertical netting a stitch woven on the vertical plane, also called Sonora weave.

visual aids magnifiers, magnifying glasses, and beading lamps with magnification lenses used to help people see better while working with small beads.

wakan a Lakota word that translates as "sacred" or "holy."

whip stitch a finishing stitch used to cover the edge of two pieces of leather or fabric with beads. It is also called wrap stitch or rolled stitch. (See Chapter 17.) In sewing terms, an overcast stitch usually refers to sewing two pieces of fabric together on the edge with thread and without beads.

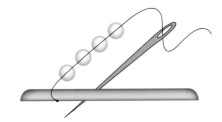

Whip Stitch

white glue water-based adhesive that is nontoxic and dries clear.

wire cutters a tool designed to cut metal like stringing wire, eye pins, and light-gauge silver.

wooden beads small pieces of wood that are shaped into beads with a hole bored through the center. Machine-made or hand-carved wooden beads are on the market.

zipper stitch a technique to turn a flat peyote piece of beadwork into a three-dimensional tube by running the needle from side to side through the pop-up beads. (See Chapter 6.)

INDEX

ABOUT THE AUTHOR

First taught by her mother, Theresa Flores Geary, Ph.D., has been creating beadwork since she was 14. She later received advanced instruction from the elders of the San Carlos Apache tribe. Although Dr. Geary once had an active career as a clinical psychologist, in the last ten years she has devoted herself to full-time beadwork, teaching classes, and promoting the art. Besides designing beaded jewelry and other beaded objects, she enjoys sharing and exchanging beading techniques and cultural histories with beaders around the world. Through her business, Mesilla Valley Beadwork, she has developed a line of bead kits sold to museums, gift shops, and retail stores throughout the United States and Canada. *Native American Beadwork: Projects & Techniques from the Southwest* (Sterling, 2003), her first beading book, has received rave reviews. Dr. Geary grew up in the Southwestern United States and boasts a proud Inter-Tribal heritage on both sides of her family. She has recently moved from the deserts of Tucson to the serene New Mexico mountain valleys, where she continues to write books about beadwork.